Acclaim for Bob Prosen's

Kiss Theory Good Bye: Five Proven Ways to Get Extraordinary Results in Any Company

"Most management/leadership books I read are confusingly complex and deliver no actionable information. Bob's book is the exception. It lays out a nuts-and-bolts map for successful execution in any business."

—KEN MAY, President and CEO, FedEx Kinko's

"If any one of the five attributes is missing, you'll never reach peak performance—no matter what business you're in."

—MAURA DONAHUE, Chairman, U.S. Chamber of Commerce

"Bob's ideas are expressed clearly and with vigor; his style is lively and provocative. He encourages executives to be both passionate and practical in their pursuit of extraordinary results. Everyone should be able to learn from Prosen's book regardless of the level or stage of business career."

—DAN T. CATHY, President and Chief Operating Officer, Chick-fil-A, Inc.

"Bob's book provides an excellent framework for increasing organizational and personal performance. Best of all, this book is down to earth and focused on operation and execution. *Kiss Theory Good Bye* is a practical, insightful way to get results."

—PETER ALTABEF, President and CEO, Perot Systems

"Will Rogers once said, 'Nothing is more common than a good idea and nothing less common than a good idea carried out.' In a hard-charging and confident manner Bob Prosen attacks head-on the problem that is at the core of so many companies' and organizations' lack of success, the glaring gap between planning and achieving the plan, and provides a crystal-clear road map to eliminating that gap."

—GARRETT BOONE, Chairman, The Container Store

"I really enjoy Bob's straight talk. His ability to cut to the chase and focus on the significant few versus the important many is right on target. This book sets the standard for getting things done!"

—JAMES PINCKNEY, General Manager, Microsoft Corporation

"Tons of wisdom! A must-read for any executive—especially those ready to take their company to the next level. Whether you're in packaged goods or capital goods, *Kiss Theory Good Bye* provides actions that will increase your company's profitability."

—JOHN SIGNORINO, CEO and President,
Chicken of the Sea International

"Insightful. Prosen captures the essence of execution. *Kiss Theory Good Bye* helps you find the right way to engage and energize your organization for measurable results. His approach made such an impact on me I hired him to train my management team."

—JOHN THOMPSON, President, Crossmark

"This work is truly a gift to leaders everywhere. I had the feeling I was stealing secrets from someone as I took notes and highlighted the many nuggets of wisdom Prosen has given us. Prosen's perceptions of what makes quality leaders and how to attain operational excellence is some of the clearest and most motivational material I have read."

—PATRICK F. QUINN, Executive Director of Operations,
Saint Paul Public Schools

"There have been many books on business leadership. However, Prosen takes the intangible and dissects it into a very precise recipe for success. I really enjoyed the comprehensive and no-nonsense approach and, in fact, think it would make a great MBA text."

—PETER THONIS, Senior Vice President, Verizon

"I must be nuts recommending Bob's darn book. If more executives were to follow and actually execute on his straightforward 'how-to' performance recommendations, guys like me would have fewer troubled companies to help lead out of the financial and operational swamps. His book is definitely unfair to turnaround folks."

—SAM COATS, President and CEO, SI Restructuring, Inc.

"*Kiss Theory Good Bye* gives chief executives the tools they need to become better leaders, become better decision makers, and get better results."

—RICHARD CARR, Vice Chairman, VISTAGE

"All the ingredients a leader must have to be successful, and more . . . the recipe to convert vision into execution!"

—SKIP MOORE, Managing Partner, Deloitte & Touche

"*Kiss Theory Good Bye* cuts through the mountain of theory and politics that bog down organizations and gives leaders simple and easy to use tools that immediately improve execution."

—DENNIS MAPLE, Executive Vice President, ARAMARK

"Unlike so many business books that focus on the past, *Kiss Theory Good Bye* provides a blueprint for guiding companies into the future. Bob Prosen has done us all a service."

—JIM DAVIDSON, Former Executive Vice President and General Manager, Hitachi Data Systems

"Bob's sharply illustrated tools and techniques will help our international architectural practice be better managed and more profitable. What our management team has learned will continue to return many times our investment."

—RALPH HAWKINS, CEO, HKS

"This is the definitive how-to book on business execution. A must-read for all experienced as well as new leaders and managers."

—ED H. BOWMAN, President and CEO, SOURCECORP

"To get results with certainty, read *Kiss Theory Good Bye*. You will discover the formula for combining the power of people and the need to get things done that will help you produce extraordinary results."

—JACK LOWE, Chairman, TDIndustries

"Regardless of the nature of your business, *Kiss Theory Good Bye* will give you specific solutions and strategies that you can begin implementing immediately to improve results."

—TED SCHWEINFURTH, Partner, Winstead, Sechrest & Minick

"Experience matters! Bob brilliantly spells out what leaders must do to produce great client, employee, and financial outcomes."

—RUSS LABRASCA, Executive Vice President, Wells Fargo Private Client Services

"Refreshingly straightforward . . . No theory here. Instead, Bob Prosen provides the playbook for getting consistent results all the time."

—KA COTTER, Vice Chairman, The Staubach Company

"Finally a book that decodes exactly what organizations must do to produce great results. All employees will benefit greatly from Bob's experience."

—DEEDRA BOULINE, VP of Organizational and Employee Development, Sabre Holdings

"Direct and to the point; Bob has done an excellent job pulling together all the essential components of execution into one place. I kept wishing I had access to this information years ago."

—AL LYNCH, Retired President and CEO, JC Penney International

"School systems committed to improving accountability will keep *Kiss Theory Good Bye* close at hand. Bob Prosen has done education a great service."

—DR. MIKE MOSES, Former Texas Commissioner of Education

"Proven principles organizations can use immediately to produce real results."

—DR. SAMUEL ROSS, Chief Medical Officer, Parkland Hospital

"Companies are always looking for ways to outperform the competition. Bob shows you how to identify and focus your entire organization on what matters most—results!"

—GARY M. DIXON, Partner, Human Capital, Ernst & Young LLP

"If you demand superior results, this is the real thing. Mr. Prosen cracks the code and gives us exactly what we want: step-by-step instructions on how to achieve results that count. Do yourself a favor. Buy it."

—WALTER JONES, Group Technology Executive, Wells Fargo Bank

"Bob is a master at building high-performance teams. He understands the importance of hiring the right people, and the importance of leadership. If you want to learn how to attract and retain top talent, read this book."

—STEVE WATSON, International Chairman, Stanton Chase International

"*Kiss Theory Good Bye* is a compelling read, offering a toolbox to public and private sector managers alike to help establish clear focus, effective management, and measurement of outcomes. In an era of rapidly diminishing resources, this is a must-read for executives to prioritize on those things that bring an organization the most value-added return on investment."

—MICHAEL A. EUGENE, Business Manager,
Los Angeles Unified School District

"An absolute must-read for senior leaders of any organization who are looking for straightforward business principles that get results!"

—MICHAEL K. BERRY, President,
HILLWOOD Properties, a Perot Company

"Bob is a compelling and inspirational speaker. His book, *Kiss Theory Good Bye*, captures his passion and is filled with focused, proven advice for getting results. Keep it close as a working business tool and reference guide."

—R. PHILLIP BOYD, CFO, OsteoMed LP

"Bob, you have a winner! I like the elegant simplicity and unique focus on how to achieve sustained profitability."

—MARK LANEY, President, Cook Children's Physician Network

"Bob's experience, proven track record, and easy-to-follow method help companies large and small achieve results that count."

—ARTURO VIOLANTE, Former President,
Greater Dallas Hispanic Chamber of Commerce

"When I first met Bob he was speaking to a group of CEOs. Bob knew exactly what I was going through running my own company. The principles in this book are right on the money! If you run a business or you own your own business, you must read this book!"

—MICHAEL RASA, President/CEO, Rasa Floors & Carpet Cleaning

"Packed with 100 percent useful information every leader should have at his or her fingertips."

—MARY SUTHER, Retired CEO,
The Visiting Nurses Association of Texas

"Every successful leader needs to read this book."

—TONY JEARY, Mr. Presentation,
author and coach to the world's top CEOs

"Strong, clear, fundamental advice for building organizations based on integrity and committed to excellence and results."

—DON FRANKLIN, Chief of Police, Addison, Texas

"Bob spells out practical, real-world examples that any company can use to get better results."

—ERIC SUDER, CEO/Founder, ESI

"Bob Prosen showed us how to work collaboratively and get results we never thought possible. His breakthrough book, *Kiss Theory Good Bye*, is a requisite read for all public and not-for-profit organizations."

—CAROL FRANCOIS, PhD, Former Chief of Staff,
Dallas Independent School District

"Bob's hit the nail square on the head! Nonprofit leaders (boards and staff) can truly move their mission forward by applying the principles he has compiled."

—LINDA L. SCHOELKOPF, President, Junior Achievement of Dallas, Inc.

Five Proven Ways to Get Extraordinary Results in Any Company

KISS THEORY GOOD BYE

BOB PROSEN

GOLD PEN™
PUBLISHING

Published by Gold Pen Publishing
18352 Dallas Parkway, Suite 136427
Dallas, TX 75287

Reprinted 2007.

Distributed by Greenleaf Book Group LP

For ordering information or special discounts for bulk purchases, please contact Greenleaf Book Group LP at 4425 S. Mo Pac Expwy., Suite 600, Austin, TX 78735, (512) 891-6100.

Cover design by R&D Thinktank
Page design and composition by Greenleaf Book Group LP

Library of Congress Control Number: 2006921936

ISBN-10: 0-9776848-0-6
ISBN-13: 978-0-9776848-0-9

Printed in the United States of America on acid-free paper

09 08 07 10 9 8 7 6 5 4 3 2

First Edition

To my mother, Edwina Joan Prosen, who always told me,
"Robert, you can do anything you want to do."

CONTENTS

PART III: EXECUTE FOR RESULTS

PREFACE

BUSINESS LEADERS NEED LESS TALK and more action! We must achieve excellent results faster, more consistently, less expensively, and without the hassles that make our jobs tedious. Whether in multinational corporations, midsize entrepreneurial businesses, or not-for-profit organizations, leaders and managers are asking, how can I get the results I need? And some dare to ask, how can I go beyond the results I need to achieve results that others think are impossible? I wrote *Kiss Theory Good Bye: Five Proven Ways to Get Extraordinary Results in Any Company* to provide the answers that business leaders and managers need to consistently achieve and even exceed their objectives.

My goal is to give you the definitive "how-to" book on business execution. It is not a compilation of rules or the collected anecdotes of other business leaders. It is my first-person account of helping to lead major companies—and some midsize ones, too—to unprecedented bottom-line results.

The how-to nature of this volume is meant to supersede the best-selling business books that explore the process of execution. Those focus mainly on what to do, whereas this book provides step-by-step instructions along with easy-to-use tools for getting unprecedented, sustainable results. Leaders want proven answers to today's business challenges. They prefer action to theory and value straightforward information that's easy to understand. Their most precious resource is time, so I condensed what matters most into actions that, when implemented, produce immediate performance improvement.

Here's how I've accumulated this information and proven advice. For twenty-five years I helped lead companies out of the status quo and into sustained profitability. These companies included Hitachi, Sprint, NCR, Sabre, AT&T, and a number of midsize companies. During that time I discovered five attributes that transform ordinary performance into extraordinary achievement.

I have analyzed the attributes that unequivocally enable an organization to consistently achieve its objectives, defined the roadblocks to building an extraordinary and profitable organization, and documented the time-tested tools and techniques I used to help management teams achieve and exceed their objectives. Many companies I've worked with are household names, while others are start-ups or privately held firms with low profiles. Almost all of these companies, regardless of size or industry, suffered from a lack of accountability. Objectives and commitments were not achieved month after month. Yet there were few consequences. Often personnel simply rationalized inferior performance, and the individual who offered the best rationalization won.

This book shows you what happens when leaders take action by asking tough questions, communicating their goals from top to bottom, establishing an accountability-based culture, and understanding that leadership and effective management are holistic endeavors. Every attribute of organizational success is inextricably linked to others.

My goal for sharing my knowledge and experiences is to give you the answers you need to immediately overcome barriers to success and enable your enterprise to achieve its full potential. Leaders want their ideas and initiatives consistently carried out without hassle and rework. They want accountability, and value results over theory. I wrote *Kiss Theory Good Bye* with two principles in mind. First, theory would be replaced with proven tools, tactics, and answers that get results. Second, all of the information must be relevant and directly applicable to today's business challenges without the need for translation.

Theory is abstract thought or contemplation that is vital because it enables speculation and testing new ideas, which become facts when proven. Theory helps us identify and solve the unknown and brings us a step closer to the future. In business, however, when it comes to execution, leaders want action and results, not theory or philosophy.

Most business leaders know what they want to accomplish and generally set clear goals and objectives. The critical missing piece is a way to quickly and consistently convert these goals and objectives into actions that produce tangible operational and financial success. *Kiss Theory Good Bye* provides the missing ingredients by revealing proven tools and actions that, when properly applied, enable organizations to cut to the chase and get what they want most—extraordinary results!

Kiss Theory Good Bye: Five Proven Ways to Get Extraordinary Results in Any Company was written for business leaders, managers, supervisors, board members, and employees who know there is a better way to do business. They intrinsically know the time-tested techniques that have produced the best results; they have the courage to readopt these techniques and implement new ones; and they have the vision to see that business as usual must change. This book reveals proven techniques to gain the extra edge over competition and execute with speed, efficiency, and maximum effectiveness.

Until now this information has only been available piecemeal, leaving you to find, assemble, and translate it to fit your business. You might have gathered some of it through mentors, by trial and error, or by surviving the "school of hard knocks." But by the time you finish reading *Kiss Theory Good Bye*, you will have the answers you need to immediately begin improving results throughout your entire organization. And you will find that this book will remain a useful resource for quick, proven answers to resolve your most pressing business challenges.

Kiss Theory Good Bye is about getting results. It takes the complexity and mystery out of business leadership. Some of what you will learn here may sound like common sense. Yet it is not common practice. Learning and consistently practicing superior leadership, sales effectiveness, operational excellence, financial management, and customer loyalty will enable your organization to achieve the results you need. The tools and tactics I share in this book have enabled top companies to report these extraordinary results:

- A worldwide travel-industry leader closed more than $100 million in sales within twenty-four months.
- A global telecom company reduced overtime 50 percent while improving on-time service delivery 33 percent.
- An international communications provider achieved 130 percent increase in productivity without adding staff.
- A major U.S. technology service company improved sales by 38 percent and exceeded its profit plan by 47 percent.
- A global travel industry vendor turned a loss of 30 percent into a profit of 21 percent in twelve months.
- A communications company increased revenue by $20M while reducing operating cost by $36 million—representing 20 percent of earnings before taxes in just eighteen months.
- A communications industry leader reduced customer service incidents by 67 percent in less than a year.
- A major U.S. technology service firm increased employee satisfaction from below 60 percent to greater than 80 percent in eighteen months.

- A global telecom provider eliminated all unsatisfactory ratings and improved customer satisfaction 39 percent within six months.
- A communications industry leader implemented a quality-improvement process and increased sales by $1.8 million.
- One of the nation's leading Internet hosting companies improved earnings by 36 percent and met EPS (earnings per share) expectations for all consecutive quarters.

These results are not unique to these companies. Your organization can achieve similar outcomes. Although I focus mostly on for-profit companies throughout this book, its principles can be readily applied to not-for-profit groups for which outcomes are just as important. In fact, some of my top clients are not-for-profit organizations. If you want to help expand awareness, serve more people, and increase giving, read on. There are many types of not-for-profit organizations that can benefit from the principles in this book:

- Schools can apply these principles to increase student completion and graduation rates, improve safety, increase test scores, raise money, allocate scarce resources, pay for performance, attract and retain qualified faculty, and communicate and work better as a team.
- Government organizations can apply these principles to reduce waste, increase motivation, improve customer service, become more efficient, attract qualified people, and eliminate poor performers.
- Churches can apply these principles to retain and increase membership, meet fund-raising goals, recruit more volunteers, and increase mission and outreach-program successes.
- Political organizations can apply these principles to increase awareness, raise money, and lead campaign organizations more successfully.

At the end of this book, in the chapter "Keep the Momentum Going," I will tell you how your organization can continue learning to achieve extraordinary results through custom-designed, organization-specific programs delivered at your business site by The Prosen Center for Business Advancement. I congratulate you on your courage to critique the past while creating the future of business practices.

ACKNOWLEDGMENTS

To my dearest wife, Sandra, NOWLYLID. Your encouragement and faith in me over the years have been the source of tremendous strength. I'm grateful to have you as my wife and best friend, and I appreciate your incredible patience and all the things you do that allow me to achieve my dreams. You are my gift, and I look forward to all that we have yet to experience.

To Matthew, Sarah, and Whitney, who are the most beautiful, loving, caring, sensitive, and brilliant children a father could ever have. My love for you is endless, and I thank you for the support and understanding you've given me through all the long hours and weekends I worked to complete this book. I am very proud of you and look forward to all the memories we have yet to create.

To my faithful schnauzer, Oreo, who brings me joy and endless companionship.

To my dear friend Janet Howe, who believed in me from the day we met. Thank you for your tireless support, the unimaginable hours and weekends you gave to help me launch my company, book, Web site, and much, much more. Your ability to transform ideas and concepts into powerful, compelling copy is nothing short of amazing. Most of all, I admire your courage to challenge my ideas and offer alternatives I never thought were possible.

To my friend and colleague Chris Ryan, for your passion, support, commitment, teamwork, long hours, and unyielding belief in our mission. Thank you for helping me exceed client expectations and create new alliances, introducing me to The Executive Committee, coordinating outstanding customer appreciation events, traveling nonstop with me across the country, being a great sounding board and company ambassador, and for the honor of working with you.

To Sally Giddens Stephenson and Peter Arnold for helping me organize my thoughts, Pam Holloway for helping me create the Five Attributes workbook, and Staci Friedel, Stephen Lynch, and Willie Baronet for your outstanding design work. To Jan Deatherage, Doug Rucker, and the entire R&D Thinktank team for creating an exceptional title and cover design. To the entire Greenleaf Book Group team for your outstanding consulting, layout, editing, marketing, and distribution. To Kevin Lofgren and Raul Sanchez for making my Web site a reality. To Gail Davis for all the great speaking engagements. To my advisory team for your honesty and courage to tell me what I needed to hear.

To all my friends and business colleagues who took time to thoughtfully critique my manuscript, help me select the right title, and offer sage advice along the way, I want to thank each of you individually: Chris Akin, Jennifer Altabef, Peter Altabef, Michael Berry, Garrett Boone, Deedra Bouline, Ed Bowman, R. Phillip Boyd, Bruce Bradford, Dan Cathy, Jim Charles, Russell Cleveland, Sam Coats, Andy Coticchio, Ka Cotter, Jim Davidson, Paul Dipp, Gary Dixon, Maura Donahue, Michael Eugene, Don Franklin, Dr. Carol Francois, Craig Hall, Ralph Hawkins, Don Hill, Tony Jeary, Walter Jones, Russ Labrasca Jr., Mark Laney, Jack Lowe, Al Lynch, Lambert Mathieu, Ken May, Leon McCaskill, Skip Moore, Tom Pace, James Pinckney, Allen Questrom, Patrick Quinn, Michael Rasa, Jim Roberts, Dr. Samuel Ross, Linda Schoelkopf, Ted Schweinfurth, Bill Sheffer, John Signorino, Drew Snow, John Steadke, Stephen Ste. Marie, Eric

Suder, Mary Suther, Craig Sutton, John Thompson, Peter Thonis, Brad Todd, Arturo Violante, Sue Wade, Bill Wallace, Steve Watson, and Jim Young.

To Dr. Jasper Arnold, Director of the Executive MBA Program at The University of Texas at Dallas School of Management, for inviting me to teach business execution as part of the Executive MBA program.

To Chris Picket and Henrietta Asriani Kristanto for your help developing and implementing The Prosen Center business effectiveness study.

To VISTAGE, formerly The Executive Committee (TEC) for allowing me the opportunity to work with hundreds of your CEOs and key business leaders across the country who are passionate about producing extraordinary bottom-line results.

To the companies I have had the pleasure to work for, including AT&T, NCR, Sprint, Sabre, Hitachi Data Systems, and all my many clients. To the thousands of employees I had the pleasure to work with, lead, and learn from over the past twenty-five years. To all my friends who support me regardless of the time it takes me to return phone calls and e-mails.

To the great leaders I have had the opportunity to work with. A few of them include Brad Boston, Joseph Gilliam, Mark Hurd, Fred Lawrence, and Gil Mauk. To Ram Charan for your thoughtful advice and to Jack Welch for your inspiration and belief that people who can execute know that winning is about results. Finally, to my mother, for making me feel loved every day and for your eternal support and encouragement. I miss your gentle touch, warm thoughts, and infinite wisdom.

KISS THEORY GOOD BYE

PART ONE

The Big Win: Maximum Profitability and Results

INTRODUCTION

Why You and Your Organization Need This Book

What are your top three objectives and how do you know you're achieving them? This may seem like a simple question, but I usually get vague generalities when leaders respond to it. Too many of them can't see the reality of their business situation because they don't even know where to start looking. They don't have a clear map to guide them to the best outcome: maximum profitability and exceptional operating results. To accomplish these goals, they need increased market share, improved earnings, employee satisfaction, and customer loyalty, along with greater operating efficiency.

Are your top three objectives quantifiable, concisely stated, and at your fingertips, so that you always know precisely how your organization is performing? Every year companies and not-for-profit organizations across the United States and around the world allocate significant resources to the development of well-thought-out plans and strategies. These documents are testaments to business acumen, cogent thinking, realistic projections, and talented management.

So why are these planned objectives so conspicuously absent in most quarterly results and bottom-line profits? You can find the answer in the glaring gap between vision and reality, between mapping the journey and arriving at the destination. Too many companies and organizations are stuck in the status quo and lack the execution tools and tactics required to convert plans into results.

Over the twenty-five years I spent helping companies achieve their financial and operating objectives, I noticed a lack of practical information to help business leaders execute their plans. Certainly there's a tremendous amount of information in the market on what other companies have accomplished. Yet what leaders really want are straightforward answers they can use immediately, without any translation, to boost their organization's performance.

Begin by answering these important questions:

- Does your company spend too much time planning and too little time executing those plans?
- Are you concerned about attracting and retaining top talent?
- Do you want to increase accountability throughout your organization?
- Are you frustrated because too many decisions end up on your desk?
- Do you spend too much time following up to ensure things get done?
- Are your competitors gaining ground?
- Are you concerned about consistently meeting your operational and financial commitments?
- Do you wonder whether your entire workforce is fully focused on meeting your organization's top objectives?
- Does your company use a defined process to reduce inefficiency and eliminate rework?

- Do you receive too much data instead of the information you need to make accurate, timely decisions?
- Are you constantly reacting to the latest crisis?

The more often you answered yes to these questions, the more you need this book's powerful information. *Kiss Theory Good Bye* includes proven instructions you can use right now to start delivering better results, from the holistic view that all attributes of a highly profitable business are inextricably linked.

Now more than ever, with the global economy and advanced technology fueling the velocity of change, it is critical for all organizations to shift their focus from simply planning and replanning to execution that achieves maximum outcomes.

The execution models I share with you are not blue-sky theories. Instead they offer specific, proven, immediately actionable techniques for removing roadblocks that limit companies to the status quo.

Why is profitability (or surplus for not-for-profit organizations) so important? Without profitability, companies cease to exist. Organizations that achieve and sustain profitability increase their value, take better care of their employees, have more options regarding risk and innovation, deliver higher satisfaction among the management team and workforce, and remain viable despite economic fluctuations. Larger surpluses enable not-for-profit groups to better meet their missions and serve more clients.

> There is another, big-picture perspective on the importance of profitability. This success helps to determine the economic strength of our nation. Companies that achieve profitability by increasing their positive net cash flow hire more people and fuel our national economy.

The fact is, however, that the majority of organizations are stuck. Sure, they all want to reach their goals faster, more efficiently, and less expensively than their competition. So what keeps them from achieving their intention?

There are five crippling habits that get companies and organizations nowhere fast:

1. Absence of clear directives
2. Lack of accountability
3. Rationalizing inferior performance
4. Planning in lieu of action
5. Aversion to risk and change

Does any of this sound familiar?

Of these, today's most prevalent business challenge is certainly the fourth roadblock, planning in lieu of action. Planning is critical to success, and successful companies are well versed in it. Yet it's the issue of execution that remains in question. What separates the winners from those who are struggling, or worse, filing for bankruptcy? The answer is the ability to execute a plan. It really is that simple.

Too often an organization's efforts are spent on politics and internal issues instead of beating the competition. Employees aren't aligned and focused on achieving their company's most critical directives. Ultimately, earnings and results suffer—which often leads to layoffs, a weakened company, and damage to the overall economy. Upon reflection, leaders frequently say they should have taken action much sooner.

To get things done, you must create change and assume risk. Most people are afraid of change. To overcome their comfort with the status quo, they have to believe that not changing will be more painful than changing. This is the turning point for getting things done.

So let's do things the right way. Throughout my career, moving up from a line manager to a CEO and now a business educator and management consultant, I have learned exactly what enables organizations to achieve exceptional outcomes and sustain profitability. I've distilled this knowledge into The Five Attributes of Highly Profitable Companies, which are the essence of this book.

THE FIVE ATTRIBUTES OF HIGHLY PROFITABLE COMPANIES

- Superior Leadership
- Sales effectiveness
- Operational excellence
- Financial management
- Customer loyalty

As you move from planning through execution and to truly sustained profitability, *Kiss Theory Good Bye* will keep you focused on critical actions you must take along the way.

Specifically, this book speaks to the following types of leaders to address issues they report as their greatest challenges.

- **Presidents, owners, CEOs, and other top leaders**, *Kiss Theory Good Bye* will show you a proven process to increase accountability, alignment, make your job easier, and make your company run more smoothly, providing you more time to plan and enjoy your personal interests while consistently meeting your company's objectives.
- **Managers and supervisors**, *Kiss Theory Good Bye* will teach you how to be recognized as a top performer, both inside and outside the enterprise. You will also learn how to align your employees to produce the results you want without a lot of conflict.
- **High-potential leaders**, *Kiss Theory Good Bye* will give you the "executive playbook" for running a successful company so that you don't waste resources by making costly mistakes while learning from the "school of hard knocks."
- **Leaders under siege**, *Kiss Theory Good Bye* will show you how to achieve the operating and financial results you need immediately to put your company back on track.
- **Leaders of start-up, merged, and fast-growing companies**, *Kiss Theory Good Bye* will teach you the process for reducing risk while dramatically increasing effectiveness

and increasing the probability that your company will consistently achieve its operational and financial objectives.

- **Board members,** *Kiss Theory Good Bye* will give you a proven method for ensuring that the organization you govern is fully accountable and meeting its most critical goals.

If you and your organization are ready to learn how to break free from the grip of the status quo and achieve extraordinary operational and financial results, then you will find *Kiss Theory Good Bye* to be a valuable and long-lasting resource. Above all, remember that executing for organizational excellence and sustained profitability is a never-ending endeavor that requires a positive mental attitude and teamwork that can only result from the buy-in of your entire organization.

I pledge to you that if you act on the directions in this book, you will achieve extraordinary results you may never have thought possible.

ACTIONS TO TAKE NOW

Start getting results immediately by taking these actions now:

- Write down and quantify your top three objectives. How do you know you are achieving them?
- Send a memo to five members of your top management team. Ask them to send you their top three objectives and the ways they know the organization is achieving them.
- Send a similar memo to five of your best middle managers. Also ask them to send you their top three objectives and the ways they know the organization is achieving them.
- Compare and contrast the responses you get from top executives and middle managers. What have you learned? What will you do to increase alignment and teamwork resulting from everyone knowing and delivering against the top three objectives?

In the next chapter, I'll explain the five crippling habits that prevent companies from achieving extraordinary results, as well as how to overcome them.

ONE

Stuck in Status Quo: Five Crippling Habits That Attack from Within

We all have excuses for our bad habits, and you'd better believe that companies and organizations are full of excuses. The following phrases may sound familiar to you: "We've tried that before and it didn't work." "I didn't make my numbers because . . ." "Here are all the things that could go wrong." "I can't get everything done." "It's not my job. It wasn't my fault." "I wish management would stop changing their minds."

Excuses signal systemic problems that are deeply embedded in the corporate culture. And while some hostile economic events are unavoidable, I find that many companies suffer from the same five crippling habits:

1. Absence of clear directives
2. Lack of accountability
3. Rationalizing inferior performance

4. Planning in lieu of action
5. Aversion to risk and change

I touched on some of these all-too-common pitfalls in the introduction. This chapter illustrates them in greater detail. In the chapters ahead, you'll learn step-by-step how to change bad habits by following a high-performance model for achieving results.

Crippling Habit 1: Absence of Clear Directives

If you're hearing or saying any of the following, then your company or organization suffers from an absence of clear directives: "I can't get anything done." "Everything is a priority." "I wish management would quit changing their minds." "I didn't know I was supposed to do that."

As a leader, you must make sure everyone who reports to you understands and stays focused on achieving the company's most important objectives, the things that matter most and must get done. Listen for what's keeping people from doing what's important. Have you set goals that are specific and measurable? Can everyone in your company articulate those goals? Do they understand how their jobs directly support those goals?

It's easy to discover the answers to these important questions. When I'm working with a company to improve operating results and profitability, one of the first things I do is walk around and ask people at all levels what the company's goals are. If they can tell me, pull it up on a computer screen, or point to a sign in their office or a break room and then describe how their work fits into the company's top objectives, my job is going to be a lot easier.

Most of the time employees don't know their employer's top objectives, and they struggle to directly connect their work to desired outcomes. Sometimes I don't even have to ask the questions, all I have to do is listen and observe. Are heads down and focused? Are people having action- and goal-oriented conversations, or are they surfing the Internet or reliving their weekends?

Of course, you can't just announce your goals and expect them to happen. For example, if improving customer loyalty by 5 percent, reaching specific production and sales goals, and increasing profitability by 2 percent are your primary objectives, not only must you make them clear, measurable, and visible, but you must also find ways to get them practiced.

Put them front and center on meeting agendas, in ongoing written and verbal communications, and in marketing collateral. Make them come to life in everything the company does. If they're just a number posted on the wall like the old Soviet quota system, then you'll just have business as usual.

You also have to be expert at saying no. There are always more things to accomplish than time and resources allow. Therefore it's management's job to help employees triage their tasks to determine what's most important to accomplish first. It's just as critical to identify what won't get done, relieving employees of less important responsibilities so the company can achieve the results that matter most.

I once reported to a senior executive who constantly frustrated me when I sent him requests requiring him to take action, and he would seldom respond. It didn't take me long to ask him why. His response was, "I only work on my top priorities and leave the rest for my organization to handle." So it was no less frustrating the next time I needed him to take action, knowing my request rested at the bottom of the pile.

Yet I had learned three important lessons. First, inform people of your priorities and what you will and won't spend time doing. Second, time is finite—we all must prioritize. Third, he expected me to lead my department. After all, I held this position because of my experience and ability. Remember why you were hired.

Goal: Align for effectiveness.

Crippling Habit 2: Lack of Accountability

If you're hearing "I would have done it but . . ." or "It's not my job," around your company, then your business is suffering from a lack of accountability.

When I find a culture of blame or a victim mentality, it often points to a lack of clear ownership and the fact that the company's reward system isn't linked to results. People need to know what they're responsible for delivering. They'll know this if you tell them directly and unambiguously. You must also reward results, and to do that you have to measure performance against clearly defined goals.

When I visit a company, I ask people what they're doing and if they know how their job fits into the company's top directives. I then ask, "How well are you performing, and how do you know?"

To be effective you must measure results against goals—not just quarterly or at year's end, but often weekly or even daily. While "meeting mania" is certainly unproductive, frequent meetings that focus on performance against those goals are absolutely necessary—and absolutely productive. Managers, along with everyone else in the company, must be held accountable. If you don't make your goals, there must be a penalty.

The best carrot and the strongest stick are often compensation. I can't believe how frequently I find that year after year workers who don't meet their objectives continue to get pay raises. If there are no consequences for poor performance, you can't expect improvement. What you can expect is a company full of poor performers.

As a leader, you must be a careful listener. There are times when people will tell you, "I would have done it but . . ." and the rest of the answer is not an excuse but a clue to If your sales force is telling you they can't mee the price is too high, dig deeper to find the r might be a weakness in your value proposition or your competitor might have a lower cost structure. It's also possible your team might not have the tools or training to make their goals.

Being able to differentiate between excuses and real problems is an essential part of management. Be responsible to people, not for them. By removing roadblocks to success, leaders enable employees to become fully responsible for delivering results.

It's easy to shift the focus of every meeting to accountability. First, require everyone to ask themselves why they're there. Can they make a difference? If not, ask them to disinvite themselves and get back to the tasks that can make a difference. Then make sure someone in the meeting captures the action items: what needs to be done, what assistance is required, who's going to do it, and by when.

Next time the team meets, start the meeting by reviewing the list of action items and commitments from the previous meeting. This will ensure progress toward the ultimate objective. When you encounter roadblocks and objectives are at risk, the entire team should address the situation proactively and make substantive offers to help. Hold people accountable, and watch results improve.

> Goal: Take ownership of results.

Crippling Habit 3: Rationalizing Inferior Performance

Whenever you hear "they," as in, "If only they would do their jobs," and "I work hard, why are they complaining?" instead of "I" in a conversation about meeting goals, you can bet someone is rationalizing by creating a defense mechanism that justifies

..erior performance. When people in a company aren't meeting their goals, but they take ownership by communicating what they require to succeed, how much it will cost, and who needs to help them, that's an example of an organization committed to results. Leaders capable of changing the focus from excuses and rationalization to removing the roadblocks that inhibit great performance should be held out as role models.

When the most productive leaders hear someone rationalizing inferior performance, they switch the conversation from negative to positive. Instead of asking why an individual hasn't met a goal, ask what he's doing to get there. Does he need help? What stands in the way? During these conversations, make certain ownership and accountability are maintained while you focus on actions required to achieve the desired outcome.

If rationalization regularly dominates discussions of performance, leaders also must ask themselves a few questions: Are you tolerant of excuses? Is there clear ownership of objectives? Are you focusing on what's most important—the significant few—or the important many? Is compensation tied to results or activity? Have you established the systems and culture to support your people in attaining their goals? Are you hiring people who are smarter than you, who can evaluate situations and offer wisdom and experience to narrow the performance gap and accelerate the attainment of objectives?

Goal: Deliver on results, not activity.

Crippling Habit 4: Planning in Lieu of Action

If only I had a nickel for every time I heard one of the following: "That's not in the plan." "We missed the plan and need a revised forecast." "I'm updating the plan to incorporate the shortfall."

When companies don't meet their profit objectives quarter after quarter, all too often everyone eventually blames the plan. Leaders then blame the employees and downsize the company. It's a vicious, disastrous, and expensive cycle.

Even though it may sound absurd, this scenario plays out frequently. Companies spend enormous amounts of time, energy, and resources on planning. They hire consultants and travel offsite to planning retreats. They bring in experts to come up with brilliant plans, and afterward, everyone feels good for a while.

The problem is that companies too often don't invest an equal amount of time, energy, and resources on achieving the results the plan targets. Instead they go through several quarters before realizing that they're not achieving the results they'd planned for, and so they say, "Let's revise the plan again."

I worked with one company that dedicated incredible resources to planning and reporting. It seemed like all they did was create reports that sat on the shelf. After a couple of months of asking what all of the reports were designed to accomplish, I determined that many of them had just grown insidiously and weren't used by anyone. Someone made a request and it was put on a to-do list, and, eventually, tremendous resources were dedicated to activities that in no way helped the company achieve its objectives. Unfortunately this unproductive and costly cycle still goes on today inside many companies.

The most effective plans are those with specific, measurable goals that are evaluated monthly. Long-range plans covering three to five years are useful for setting and communicating direction and should be restricted to senior management. Short-range plans covering twelve to eighteen months are what leaders need most to remain on course and manage results. For more information on plans, refer to chapter 7.

Plans and associated measurements must focus on simple-to-articulate goals owned by specific people. The measurement system has to be visible weekly, or in some cases even daily, so that everyone knows the results and understands the deviations. When deviations occur—and they will—a company must act immediately to remedy the situation. Problems never get better without action. They only grow worse.

Critical projects such as software development and deployment of new systems and major capital construction projects are a few examples of instances where important measurements have to be managed closely. If progress in any area falls behind plan, immediate action is required to minimize the impact and to regain lost ground. Key measures include percent of project completed compared to percent of budget spent; number of milestones completed on schedule compared to plan; product/service revenue compared to plan; and expense as a percent of revenue. The more important the outcome, the tighter the results have to be managed. For more information on business metrics, refer to chapter 10.

Goal: Focus on delivery and execution.

Crippling Habit 5: Aversion to Risk and Change

How do you like this excuse: You're new to a company, you have some great ideas for improvements, you share them, and then you get shot down with, "Once you know what we're facing, you'll understand why we do things this way."

In other words, once you become a part of the problem, you won't want to shake things up.

It's true we're all creatures of habit. We'd much rather navigate familiar territory and clutch the belief that if we just keep doing what we've done that produced good results, those outcomes will continue in perpetuity. Of course, that theory is ridiculous, because the world around us is in constant flux.

What's even more ridiculous is that many businesses just keep doing things that have produced *bad* results, always expecting a different outcome. They become expert at rationalization and maintain that way of thinking until something dramatic happens to the business. Sometimes the higher up you go in an organization, the more prevalent this behavior becomes. Why? Because senior people believe they have more to protect, so they don't want to risk losing anything.

Picture an old dog lying on the porch, moaning. "What's wrong with your dog?" a visitor asks the owner. "Well, he's lying on a nail, but it doesn't hurt quite enough to make him get up," the owner replies.

It's the same in business—the pain of change must be perceived as less than the pain of maintaining the status quo. Until this condition is met, little will change.

Most companies wait too long to change. They delay until there is no other choice. We see it every day. Companies are taking high write-offs, reducing their workforces, cutting benefits, dividends, and earnings expectations, then finally resorting to change because their competition has beaten them or they are facing a financial crisis. Not-for-profit organizations that react too slowly end up cutting services, depleting surpluses, reducing their staff, and receiving fewer donations.

In addition to a culture of excuses and rationalization, another symptom of aversion to risk is meeting mania. If a company is gridlocked in too many meetings, then someone in that company is afraid to make a decision. That someone is usually at the top, and, unfortunately, this behavior trickles all the way down through middle management to the line workers.

People want to work for leaders who have the guts to make a decision and stick with it. If your company holds meetings with lots of people to gain broad political consensus, then a leader is trying to ensure that if something goes wrong, there will be plenty of people to blame.

Instead, management must encourage calculated risk taking and truly demonstrate that people who take risks and occasionally miss the mark will live to try again. A culture of blame, fear, and meeting mania can't flourish in that healthy environment. Gains in productivity alone are reason enough to put a halt to unnecessary meetings.

What leaders must communicate by example is that calculated risk taking, seeking expert advice, assessing the pros and cons, making a decision, and then vigorously moving forward are the behaviors that earn rewards.

> Goal: Remain competitive and flexible.
> Don't get trapped in the status quo.

So now that you understand what often goes wrong in business, how do you fix it?

I have learned exactly what enables companies and organizations to consistently achieve their objectives and sustain profitability. In the next chapter, I'll discuss the foundation of my high-performance execution model based on The Five Attributes of Highly Profitable Companies.

ACTIONS TO TAKE NOW

Before proceeding, begin learning about these proven execution models by taking these actions now:

1. List your three worst work habits.
2. Write down your management team's three worst habits.
3. What steps will you take to address your habits and what requests will you make of your team to improve theirs?
4. How can you make the culture more welcoming to change?
5. How do you know rewards are tied to measurable results throughout the organization?
6. Schedule two walkabouts per month to ask employees what they are working on and to see how well they are performing.

PART TWO

The Five Attributes of Highly Profitable Companies

TWO

Superior Leadership: The Relentless Pursuit of Vision and Results

---

Superior leaders develop the vision and have the courage to make decisions. They must be entrepreneurial, know what's essential, take risks, and encourage others to do the same. They must know how to access the truth and build a culture based on ownership and accountability while living with ambiguity. They must have fearless determination and perseverance and be passionate about results. And they must always put the company first and understand that people are their most important asset.

To accelerate profitability and results, which should be every company's ultimate goal, you must understand the attributes that are consistently found in the most successful, highly profitable enterprises. Whether they're service oriented or product based, privately owned, publicly traded, or not-for-profit, thriving companies have certain common characteristics that enable them to achieve operational and financial success. I've synthesized five ways that set leading companies and organizations apart from followers. I call them The Five Attributes of Highly Profitable Companies:

1. Superior leadership
2. Sales effectiveness
3. Operational excellence
4. Financial management
5. Customer loyalty

This chapter discusses superior leadership and how it is the fundamental driver of profitability and success. While there is abundant information on the market about leadership, this chapter provides you with the most important aspects of superior leadership as they apply to achieving extraordinary operational and financial results.

How do you recognize a superior leader? The answer is simple: a true business leader has the ability to continually meet or exceed a company's operating and profitability objectives. Follow this model and it will lead you to the results and profits you desire.

This is the single most important job a leader has, because the ability to achieve and accelerate results and profitability often means the difference between calamity and cash flow. Without increasing positive net cash flow, companies cannot take care of their employees, customers, and shareholders, or give back to society. Public and not-for-profit organizations that do not meet their goals and objectives and fail to fulfill their charter ultimately find themselves with new leadership or forfeit control to their governing body.

The Prosen Center for Business Advancement conducts a series of business effectiveness studies. In this book I have included highlights from the most recent business effectiveness studies in which the top executives of sixty-six companies, ranging in size from $2 million to $2 billion and spread across twenty industries, rated themselves and their enterprises on twenty-one leadership dimensions. The findings revealed the following strengths and weaknesses.

Strengths

- We encourage open communications and full disclosure: 89 percent.
- We have regular performance reviews: 73 percent.
- The top objectives of my company have been clearly defined and articulated: 70 percent.
- We take action to solve problems immediately: 63 percent.
- I consistently hire and surround myself with people who are smarter than I am: 61 percent.

Weaknesses

- There is ample time to plan: 17 percent.
- We consistently meet commitments without having to follow up: 27 percent.
- We only have meetings when they make sense—when we have clearly defined objectives that are tied to the company's top objectives: 31 percent.
- I get quality reports that show me exactly what I need in order to make smart decisions: 34 percent.
- We consistently achieve our growth and profitability objectives: 37 percent.

To evaluate your organization's leadership effectiveness and instantly compare your results to those of all other participating companies, go to www.bobprosen.com/leadershipeffectiveness. The evaluation process is free, completely automated, and absolutely anonymous.*

* Please note that this study is designed specifically for leaders and managers with direct reports. It is not designed for individual contributors.

Because the ability to execute is vital to the company's overall success, I encourage leaders and managers to conduct the same study off-line within their organization. They will learn if their management team supports their view of how well the enterprise executes. They will also then have access to specific information they can use to improve results by enhancing strengths and improving areas of weakness.

Think about where you and your company fit within the superior leadership strengths and weaknesses of this particular self-assessment. How would you rate yourself? How would you rate your company? Whatever your rankings, the following discussion offers proven ways to achieve superior leadership.

Remember that these results are from senior leaders. When managers and supervisors within companies and organizations answer these same questions, it's very common to see a gap between the leader's view and that of the managers and supervisors.

In order to compare and contrast how business leaders and employees view some of the same issues, I have included findings from a Harris Interactive poll, commissioned by Franklin Covey, of more than twelve thousand full-time employees. (The word *Harris* precedes Harris Interactive poll results placed throughout this book.)

Harris:

- Organizational strategy and goals are precisely understood: 48 percent.
- My organization has decided what its most important goals are: 58 percent.
- Everyone has clear, measurable, deadline-driven work goals: 45 percent.
- My individual work goals are translated into daily tasks and activities: 54 percent.

- Time spent executing top goals: 60 percent.
- We hold ourselves accountable for reaching our commitments on time: 58 percent.

Note that 70 percent of the business leaders say their company's top objectives have been clearly defined and articulated. Yet only 48 percent of employees say they understand the organization's strategy and goals.

Now that you have had a chance to evaluate your organization's leadership effectiveness, let's shift focus to how superior leaders achieve results.

Learn to Lead

Certainly, some people are born leaders, yet we can all learn to be better leaders by selecting the best role models and surrounding ourselves with the right people. In the context of this book and our quest to achieve extraordinary operating and financial results, the following leadership characteristics emerge as key.

Inspire Loyalty and Trust

It's the Golden Rule: Do unto others as you would have them do unto you. In other words, to inspire loyalty and trust in others, a leader actually must *be* trustworthy and loyal. This is easy to say and certainly harder to do, given the many hidden political agendas that dwell in most companies and organizations. Remember, everything you say and do as a leader is constantly being evaluated by your employees and external constituencies. Therefore you must continuously demonstrate uncompromising integrity in all your actions and communications, including those that are nonverbal.

A powerful way to build trust and loyalty is to make and meet commitments. Organizations that treat commitments as promises and deliver results without follow-up build deep bonds and tremendous esprit de corps. Trust also allows leaders to delegate with confidence, thereby allowing them more time to think, plan, and move the company ahead. Superior leaders delegate well rather than following up and doing things themselves that are better left to others. This may be particularly challenging for entrepreneurs who are used to controlling every aspect of the business.

> *Harris:* We hold ourselves accountable for achieving our commitments on time: 58 percent.

One of the chief characteristics a leader must have is the ability to find the truth. Companies and organizations expect leaders to know how to confirm the truth before accepting it or taking action. Often there is more than one version of any issue, and it's the leader's role to ferret out the facts. This means not always accepting the first answer or statement you hear and not necessarily agreeing with the last person you speak with. When it comes to important decisions, it's imperative to first validate the facts and situation.

After graduating from engineering school, I accepted a job with AT&T Long Lines. I was one of thirteen people hired that year for the Management Development Program. The program was designed to develop high-potential future leaders. The program's most attractive aspects were the opportunity to work in many different departments and the possibility of eventually becoming a general manager. My first few years were both exciting and challenging. Then one day I was called to the division manager's office and told he was removing me from the program because "I made the job look too easy." Initially I didn't understand his decision. Why would someone be penalized for top performance? But with time, I finally understood that he felt threatened. In those days AT&T was a regulated monopoly, and the culture was one of "go along to get along." I didn't fit the mold. Instead, I always looked for ways to make things better. Needless to say, I was devastated by his decision. Several days later, Joe Gilliam, regional vice president and the division manager's boss, called and asked me to move from Dallas to Kansas City to join his staff. Obviously, I was skeptical and didn't want to risk relocating my family to a new city only to part company shortly thereafter. Joe's offer was the beginning of a deep friendship built solely on trust. I accepted his offer after he agreed to reinstate me in the program and promote me to district manager if I performed up to his expectations. I threw myself into the job, and within a year I was promoted and my career soared. Joe and I both took risks, made commitments, and followed through. That's what trust and loyalty are all about.

Hire Smart

One of the most important aspects of being a superior leader is hiring people smarter than you. The difference between good performance and great performance is not just having smart people, but also having the right great people in the right positions. That's why top leaders spend more time putting the right team in place to accomplish their objectives than they spend on planning, strategizing, or many other components of their job.

Often ineffective leaders have a fear of not knowing the answer to every question. They personally want to bring all relevant facts to the table every time. That's not only impossible but also counterproductive. Effective leaders hire people who can provide the answers that are pertinent to their particular area of expertise. True leaders also know how to listen to advice and move out of the way to let others do what they do best.

When I was brought in to lead a division of NCR's professional services organization, I realized I had my work cut out for me. We had to change the culture from being response driven to that of a proactive solutions provider. One of my first initiatives was to assess my team, making certain the right people were in the right positions. After a few months our team was in place. It was made up of a combination of internal talent and a couple of people hired from the outside. As a team, our goal was to become the top-performing division within eighteen months. Once that was achieved, I promised myself I would make time to sit by the pool every Friday afternoon to think, plan, and move the organization ahead to ensure we maintained the gain. I enjoyed months of free Fridays, and by investing reflective time to analyze, create, and plan, we exceeded our projected gain.

As a team, we increased sales 38 percent while achieving the firm's highest profit level and employee satisfaction rating.

Here are a few more examples of why it's important to hire people smarter than you. While at Sprint, I left the director of capacity planning position open for many months until I found the absolute best person. I took a lot of heat from senior management, but decided not to compromise and held out until I eventually hired one of the top pros in the business. Not only did my job get easier, but we were also able to make better strategic and financial decisions. I followed the same approach when I hired Ken Pederson at Sprint and Lambert Mathieu at Sabre. We worked so well together that I took them with me to several other companies, where they flourished and continue to make a difference.

I have also made my share of staffing mistakes. One of the biggest mistakes was placing the wrong person in charge of the contingency planning department to develop methods and procedures in the event of a disaster. In retrospect, I should have taken more time up front to review the employee's past performance and speak with his previous managers and peers before promoting him. After a few months, I noticed critical assignments weren't getting done and the employee kept blaming others instead of taking responsibility. For the next two months I tried coaching him to no avail, and eventually I exited him from the business. The entire process took six months to conclude and put us way behind plan. The disruption to the organization, along with the added work and stress necessary to closely manage a performance problem, far exceeded the time it would have taken to hire the right person in the first place.

Early in my career I worked far too many hours and followed up on every detail only to fall short of meeting some important objectives. I realized how important it is to hire people who knew more about their area of expertise than I did. When you surround yourself with experts, you create a body of knowledge that's far superior to that of one expert surrounded by worker bees. This body of knowledge will increase the velocity of your progress and propel you more quickly toward your goal than you ever thought possible.

When I meet with company leaders, I ask for a show of hands from those who hire people smarter than themselves. Many hands go up. Then I ask how they know, and the hands begin to drop.

So how do you determine if you have hired the right people? First, ask yourself how often the people around you recommend sound ideas that you never knew were possibilities. Does this happen once a week? Once a month? Does it ever happen?

If you're hiring people who are smarter than you, you should be surprised with their new ideas and solutions. You should be constantly learning from them.

Second, in the privacy of your office, study each person in your organization who reports to you, and ask yourself, if there were no ramifications associated with the answer, would I pick this person again to be on my team and in the same position? Caution! If you worry about what you would do if the answer is no, you will not answer the question honestly.

If you can answer *often* to the first question and *yes*, without hesitation, to the second, then you have the right person in the right job. When you hire first-class professionals, your job will get easier and your objectives will be achieved faster, better, and more profitably.

One of the toughest jobs for a leader is hiring someone you don't know. The last thing we want is to hire wrong and then have to deal with the aftermath. Here is a secret I use to increase the probability of making the right hiring decision: During the latter stages of the interviewing process, after my colleagues and I have met with the prospective hire several times, I ask the candidate to write a one-page action plan describing what he or she will do the first sixty days on the job. The next time we meet, I ask the person to present the plan. This not only allows me to evaluate the candidate's style, approach, and critical thinking skills, but it also gives me a ready-made performance plan by which to evaluate the person in the months to come. If I'm hiring to fill a senior position, I ask for a three-month action plan.

Foster a Healthy Corporate Culture

To create and maintain the right corporate culture is any leader's greatest challenge. It demands acute, ongoing attention to morale, attitudes, and exemplary employee performance. Simply put, culture is the way things get done, and it encompasses both the spoken and unspoken rules of the game.

Unfortunately politics are unavoidable in business, and the bigger the company, the more politics are present. But politics are the archenemy of a healthy culture. More quickly than anything else, politics will kill the spirit of teamwork and divert the focus from the company's primary objectives. Therefore, a superior leader must root out politics wherever and whenever they arise and call a halt to political behavior in a pointed and public way. Let everyone know that you won't tolerate political maneuvers.

Harris: We make decisions based on the best ideas and information rather than on office politics: 39 percent.

Some of my clients respond that politics are inevitable, that people are political and you can't do anything about it.

Sure I can, and so can you. People are social, but they aren't necessarily political. A true leader can shape an organization's culture so that politics are minor and teamwork to reach shared goals is paramount.

Here's a typical scenario: You're in a meeting, trying to reach consensus. You finally unite everyone in agreement. Then, after the meeting, you begin to hear hedging. Some of those who agreed in the public venue are privately expressing doubt.

The solution is to immediately recall those who were in the meeting and bring dissenting opinions into the open for debate. Then when everyone is realigned, make it clear that when you leave the meeting you expect everyone to unilaterally support the decisions in every conversation with every employee. A healthy culture grows from honest, open communication, not closed-door, behind-the-scenes politics.

Harris:

- We do not undermine each other: 37 percent.
- People avoid blaming others when things go wrong: 30 percent.

I always ask leaders if they are willing to do what it takes to ensure that all of their employees are focused on meeting or exceeding the leaders' most critical business goals. Sounds impossible to do, right? But it's doable with an all-out commitment to a healthy corporate culture. The most important aspects of a healthy culture are establishing clear objectives, effective communication, implementing an accountability-based leadership model focused on results instead of activity, eliminating victim mentality, minimizing politics, proactive teamwork, establishing effective measurements and rewards, and mastering personal involvement in day-to-day aspects of the business.

When it comes to executing for results, accountability is your primary driver. Profitability and results start by assigning clear ownership to every aspect of the business.

A superior leader is direct and forthright with people in every conversation, letting them know where they stand, what's needed from them, and when it is needed. Often good leaders can become great leaders by reshaping the way they talk.

When you make a request of someone, take a little extra time to explain why you are making it. Put it in context and explain why it's important to the goals of the business. Then the person can provide a more robust solution because she understands the purpose of the task and how the information will be used. Ask what the person needs to complete the task. This approach removes excuses, reduces rework, and is a great way to build relationships. It's also a great way to develop future leaders by increasing responsibility and encouraging decision making and creativity. By holding others accountable, you are teaching them to accept responsibility.

When you follow an accountability-based leadership model, based on clear objectives and clear measurements, it exposes the effectiveness—and ineffectiveness—of your company at all levels. Results speak for themselves, and they speak volumes. Those who achieve their objectives and treat people fairly along the way can be targeted to play increasingly important roles in the business.

It's easy to determine whether your organization has an accountability-based culture. Just listen to the conversation going on in meetings. Is conversation directed toward commitment? Are individuals talking about what is important and what will and won't get done? Are they making requests of one another and asking for commitments? Or do conversations stray to generalities, vagueness, rationalization, and missed expectations?

Do you have people who constantly talk about how hard they work, how many hours they put in, how little vacation they take, yet you wonder what they actually produce? If so, most often these people are focused on activities instead of results. They will continue to do this as long as your culture condones this behavior.

I know a group is performing well when they talk about actual results, not the activities and hurdles along the way. When team members hold themselves accountable, you hear responsibility in their conversations. They ask one another for help in order to get on track. There are no victims, excuses, or concerns over a lack of knowledge. Instead they are searching for the knowledge and support they need from everyone around the table to reach the company's goals.

Superior leaders work diligently to maintain company-wide focus on management's most critical business goals and to see these goals become results.

To maintain this type of focus on a company's critical path to results and profitability, leaders must first provide clear direction that is concise and easy to understand. Do you want to dramatically increase the probability of success while reducing mistakes, rework, and unnecessary expense? If so, then clearly state objectives and make specific requests based on those objectives. As a result, employees will know what's expected of them, because you have told them directly and unambiguously.

> What would your life be like if your company continually met or exceeded top management's objectives? At a minimum, you would have more time to plan and enjoy more of life's pleasures.

It's easy to determine whether or not the company is focused on the most critical business goals. Just walk around and ask individual employees what the company's top business goals are and what they are doing today to accomplish them.

If one of the top goals is to increase profit by 2 percent over the previous year, you should expect to hear responses similar to the following when you ask how a particular department is helping the company accomplish its goal:

- **Human resources:** We are revising the commission plan to increase sales of higher-margin products by 20 percent.
- **Finance:** We are refining the labor-reporting system to more accurately calculate individual product margins by the end of the first quarter.
- **Sales:** We are training our salespeople on the new customer credit screening process to help reduce bad debt by 10 percent.
- **Customer service:** We are determining the root causes of all warranty claims to reduce the amount by 20 percent.
- **Manufacturing:** We are reducing the cost of waste 15 percent by selling production by-products and scrap to the secondary market.

Simply listen to their responses.

Superior leaders must also provide measurement tools required to keep the company constantly moving toward its top objectives. With proper measures in place, every employee should be able to answer *yes* to the question, Did my actions today move the company closer to achieving our most critical business goals?

Master Communicators

A first-rate leader must clearly communicate and integrate company objectives with the culture and then delegate responsibility.

Micromanaging is often evidence of the need to delegate more effectively and strengthen trust and accountability. Here, the lesson is to keep important information flowing. Have you ever worked in a company where employees said they were given too much information?

I've never heard an employee say, "Stop providing me with meaningful information. I have all I need."

I once worked for Fred Lawrence, executive vice president for Sprint, who was a master communicator. He made sure everyone was informed by holding regular all-management meetings to discuss status and important updates. Whenever he would discuss a topic that involved your area of responsibility, he would ask you to elaborate and participate directly in the discussion. He would also call you up to ask for your advice before making key decisions. Fred made himself very visible to employees by holding skip-level meetings and by traveling to remote locations to speak directly with field personnel. He made you feel like an insider, and he trusted people with important information. He also shot straight and offered encouragement even when delivering bad news.

There are too few leaders like Fred Lawrence. Instead, I continually hear employees say they don't know the company's top objectives, and exactly what they are supposed to do to accomplish them, or they don't understand why management asks them to focus on one aspect of the business as opposed to another.

Harris: All workers are focused on organizational goals: 53 percent.

In fact, top management rarely visits with employees to discuss issues and communicate objectives in order to find out what is really going on. If the questions, Why did I have to read about it in the paper? and Why was I the last to know? sound familiar to you, then you aren't sharing enough of the right information with your employees. The most important aspects of effective communication are the following:

- Members of management who view themselves as teachers
- Clarity, honesty, candor, and the ability to listen
- Prioritized objectives that focus on the significant few versus the important many
- Relentless communication of the company's top objectives
- Refusing to allow the company to be run by the rumor mill
- Management that remains visible and interacts with all levels of employees

When you believe you are communicating enough, communicate more. Successful companies are filled with great people making commitments to fulfill objectives, all linked through effective communications.

How well you communicate will influence the results you achieve. Keep the following information in mind as you determine the best ways to communicate.

Tips on How People Learn and Remember People retain the following:

- 10 percent of what they read
- 20 percent of what they hear
- 30 percent of what they see
- 50 percent of what they see and hear
- 70 percent of what they say and write
- 90 percent of what they say and do*

* Dale's "Cone Experience" Data, taken from Winman & Meirhenry Educational Media, Charles Merrill, 1969

Recognize and Reward Excellence

Nothing undermines dedication and high-level performance more directly than being unrecognized or unappreciated. Establishing clear performance measures that ensure full accountability are the foundation of recognizing excellence. This is a fundamental tenet of superior leadership because it helps you keep the right people in the right jobs. If you don't recognize and reward excellence, the best people will move on to a company or organization that shows them the appreciation they deserve. The lesson here is simple: the greatest rewards go to the people who have performed the best against measurable objectives.

Harris:

- I feel that my contributions to achieving our goals are recognized and appreciated: 45 percent.
- Rewards and consequences are clearly based on performance measures: 30 percent.

Here is a real example of tying rewards to results. After the break-up of the Bell System, access costs became one of the biggest problems for long-distance carriers, representing almost 50 percent of revenue. Deregulation required local telephone companies to charge long distance carriers a fee for using their facilities to originate and complete long-distance calls. The costs were enormous and the billing processes were new and fraught with errors, which lead to significant disputes. My first position with Sprint was managing and forecasting these costs. After a few months it became clear that many departments had to work together to get the process under control. Therefore, I created a cross-functional team of almost fifty people whose goal was to reduce cost by at least $30 million. To gain buy-in and commitment, I designed a bonus program that would compensate the team for achieving the goal. After approximately six months of tireless work, the team reduced the cost of access by $36 million. To reward the team, I had the senior vice president of the department personally hand out checks ranging from $2,000 to $9,000 depending on each employee's contribution. That was also the year the company posted its first profit. To learn other ways to reward employees, I highly recommend Bob Nelson's *1001 Ways to Reward Employees*.

Superior leaders who encourage hard work, yet only reward results, are responsible *to* people and not *for* them, are hard on performance and easy on the people, give credit, and accept fault. Once this thinking becomes the standard, you will find your company or organization filled with great performers.

Be Decisive

Essential to leadership are the ability and courage to make decisions. Nothing frustrates employees more than indecisiveness. Employees want leaders to take a stand and make decisions so they can get on with their work. Senior leaders tend to make fewer decisions. However, their decisions are often more important and have greater impact on the business. One of the best ways to mitigate risk before making important decisions is to involve key people, both on and off the team, to get advice and discuss alternatives. Once this is done, it's the leader's responsibility to decide.

Throughout my career I have made many tough decisions. Often the hardest decisions involved people. These include deciding if someone should be promoted; deciding how to deal with performance problems, force reductions, employee complaints, and terminations; making the correct hiring decision; and handling counter offers.

There also are critical business decisions that, depending on the outcome, can limit your career. I remember being faced with one such decision at Sprint. I had to decide if we would break from tradition and invest in a Hitachi Data Systems mainframe computer. I remember presenting the financial savings to the chairman and him saying, "You better be right." Thankfully, the installation was flawless and Sprint became one of Hitachi Data Systems' largest customers.

On another occasion, as district operations manager for AT&T, I had a tough choice to make. We were installing coast-to-coast fiber-optic cable against an almost impossible time schedule. For engineering reasons the cable had to be buried at a certain depth. Somewhere in Alabama we ran into a long stretch of rock in the cable's path, requiring a special machine to cut a trench to the appropriate depth. The installation crew determined it would take too long, so they decided to encase the cable in steel pipe and leave it above ground until it could be buried properly. When I learned of the decision I instructed the team to bury the cable properly now rather than risk a service interruption later. This decision was met with a lot of resistance because the added time to do it right would jeopardize the installation due date. Nonetheless, I stuck with my decision and alerted senior management to the possible delay. I had to decide whether making the due date was more important than protecting thousands of customers from a potentially extended service interruption. Thankfully, the crew worked extra hard and we met the installation date.

Maintain a Holistic View of the Business

Taking a comprehensive view of business is critical. We all appreciate leaders who understand the ramifications of their decisions and the reality that a decision in one area will impact all other areas. This holistic view is another key attribute of superior leadership. Leaders must understand that the entire organization has to win—not just any one unit. That's why superior leaders work *on* the process, not *in* the process. They are aware of the whole process from start to finish and are concerned about end-to-end performance.

As a result, they focus on streamlining every aspect of the operation to make it perform as efficiently and profitably as possible. Then they allocate resources appropriately, and step back to watch the machine in motion. Leaders ensure that everyone works as a team and don't allow one part of the business to win at the expense of another.

I once worked for Ralph Stewart, senior vice president and general manager of Sabre. Ralph had the ability to see the entire landscape and call on different functional areas within the company to work together to ensure achievement of common objectives. He knew when to escalate issues, who to get support from, and exactly what was needed from each department to maximize results. He also knew how to access the truth and hold people accountable, and he wasn't afraid to make tough and sometimes unpopular decisions.

While at Sabre, I was faced with a tough choice. One of our industry segments was losing money. Thankfully, our financial system clearly identified the problem. After careful analysis, we only had two options: to renegotiate several client contracts or exit the industry. Following approval from the CEO, I set out to renegotiate the contracts. After several long negotiations, we decided to wind down the projects and ultimately exit the market. This was a particularly difficult decision because we had been in the industry for many years and couldn't find a way to be profitable.

Superior leaders always put the company first and focus on what's right for the business. They maintain an effective balance between planning and doing. In the end, one of the greatest compliments a leader can receive is to be respected. This evaluation is hard to achieve unless you lead in a fair, balanced, and holistic way.

Does Your Leadership Team Measure Up?

In my workshops, to help companies evaluate their own leadership teams, I teach leaders and managers how to ask key questions that should each be answered with a resounding *yes!* Here are nine of the most important statements you can use to evaluate the effectiveness of your leadership team:

1. The top objectives of my company have been clearly defined and articulated.
2. Everyone in my company knows the top objectives and understands what is expected of them.
3. There are appropriate incentives for producing results and penalties for not producing results.
4. We have regular performance reviews.
5. I consistently hire and surround myself with people who are smarter than I am.
6. We consistently achieve our business and profitability objectives.
7. There is ample time to plan.
8. We only have meetings when they make sense—when we have clearly defined objectives that are tied to the company's top objectives.
9. We consistently meet commitments without follow-up.

Very Important Lessons

Over the years, working with many different companies, I have learned some characteristics that ultimately make a superior leader a strong contributor to achieving and accelerating profitability:

- Consistently exceeds profitability objectives
- Demonstrates relentless pursuit of vision and results

- Demonstrates an unyielding commitment to the business
- Faces tough realities and avoids excuses and rationalization
- Recognizes the important distinction between profit and cash flow versus revenue and growth
- Surrounds himself/herself with experts
- Knows how to find the truth
- Develops an early-warning system to identify problem areas
- Acts quickly to overcome problems as they arise
- Knows the details
- Is decisive
- Is ethical, fair, and consistent
- Runs leaner than the management team would prefer
- Raises more money than the management team needs
- Is always learning
- Has a support group

Moving On

With a foundation of superior leadership, you're almost ready to move on to the second key attribute of highly profitable companies—sales effectiveness. Indeed, if you think about your business as an economic machine, with superior leadership as the driver, then sales is the fuel.

ACTIONS TO TAKE NOW

But before you move on, here are some actions to take now:

1. Write down the three most important ways for you to improve your leadership abilities along with key milestones and dates for achieving them.
2. What are the three most important ways for your managers to improve their leadership abilities? How and when will you communicate this to each member on your team?
3. How can your company or organization communicate better with its employees and with its stakeholders?
4. Who needs to delegate better? How can you get him or her to do that?
5. Do you have the right people in the right positions? If not, what actions are you prepared to take to accomplish this?
6. Does the company or organization make and meet commitments without having to follow up? If not, what actions will you take to make this a reality?

THREE

Sales Effectiveness: Your Company's Lifeline

Profitable revenue is the lifeblood of a company and can solve many challenges. Therefore, devote significant resources to ensuring your company develops realistic forecasts and consistently meets its sales plan. It's much more enjoyable and a lot easier to achieve and maintain sustained profitability by meeting the top line instead of cutting costs.

This chapter focuses on the second of The Five Attributes of Highly Profitable Companies—sales effectiveness. Sales are key to profitability because a healthy revenue stream can solve many problems within a company. Creating a strong sales organization is both a science and an art. And the great thing is, there's no mystery about the path to success. Sales are one of the most objective aspects of business because they are measurable by numbers. You either make your desired numbers or you don't, and if you don't, you must continue to make changes until you do. There are several key steps that any sales organization can follow to success.

The surveys conducted by The Prosen Center for Business Advancement on business effectiveness include measures of sales effectiveness. In one recent study the senior leaders of more than sixty companies rated themselves and their enterprises on this subject. The findings revealed the following strengths and weaknesses:

Strengths

- Salespeople involve senior management to help close important new business: 85 percent.
- Salespeople have in-depth knowledge of the competition and know how to differentiate themselves: 61 percent.

Weaknesses

- We recruit great salespeople instead of teaching people how to sell: 14 percent.
- We have a clear definition of all selling stages and win-probability definitions: 28 percent.
- There is a formal process to remove internal obstacles that impede sales: 28 percent.
- There is a process to replicate top sales successes and to teach lessons learned: 30 percent.

Think about where you and your company fit within these strengths and weaknesses. How would you rate yourself? How would you rate your organization?

Create New, Profitable Customers for Life

The primary expectation of any sales organization is to continually create new, profitable customers who are in solid financial shape and can develop into long-term relationships—customers for life. It's important for salespeople to understand that not all customers are good customers. Instead, salespeople must use due diligence to identify the right customers for the company.

I can't stress enough the importance of qualifying prospective customers. It's essential for the sales organization to screen customers early in the process. To do this, they should verify budgets; pin down the timing of the sale and when it will close; identify the customer's sense of urgency; determine and follow the correct approval process; deal with the "real" decision makers throughout the process; and, most importantly, establish the customer's creditworthiness.

If you don't take these steps early in the sales process, you reduce the probability of winning, waste precious resources, and, worst of all, acquire customers you can't serve properly or who end up not paying.

Establish Strong Quota and Ethical Standards

A successful sales organization worships its quotas and adheres to the highest ethical standards regardless of competitive pressures. Companies that are passionate about results understand that quotas and standards are commitments that have to be met consistently and methodically every week and every month, not in fits and starts. Certainly there may be interruptions in sales patterns, a month or two in which sales are off, or even a slow quarter. Yet if sales quotas go unmet week after week, month after month, then the company needs to hold itself accountable.

> Leaders must listen carefully and evaluate what the sales force is telling them. Is the price too high? Is there a problem with product quality, delivery, or customer service? Does the company need to reevaluate its value proposition?

Too many companies rationalize poor performance and ultimately accept being behind plan. When this happens, take immediate action, because missing the top line has a domino effect through the entire company. Great salespeople love the success of selling and feel disenfranchised when they don't achieve their goals. If they believe the company is holding them back, they'll move on to another organization where they can succeed. So, it's management's job to be aware of what's keeping excellent salespeople from doing a great job.

When there are real problems, management must remove the roadblocks to sales success. Management should put the necessary tools and processes in place so that the only factor left to determine success is each salesperson's ability to sell—to find and close business. There should be no reason for excuses. The best way to achieve a "no excuses" culture is for management to work hand in hand with the sales organization to determine the root cause of any issues inhibiting quota attainment so they can be removed permanently. This is a never-ending responsibility. It requires management's ongoing attention and personal involvement to ensure that all roadblocks are immediately exposed and overcome.

> *Harris:* Systems and processes are aligned to help us achieve our goals: 38 percent.

If management has done its job but excuses are still being voiced about not meeting quotas—such as, "The price is too high," "We don't have the features that our competition has," "We don't have the right relationships," and "Donors have reduced funding"—then it's time to weed out those salespeople who don't meet quotas consistently. This is one of the few areas in business that's virtually black-and-white. If salespeople have been trained, have the tools and support required to understand and communicate the product or service to the market, and they still aren't achieving quotas, remove them from the sales organization immediately. Waiting and hoping for improved performance only increases the odds of not achieving the company's top line. Pay close attention to this critical business area. Most leaders wait too long to take action.

To ensure that quotas are achieved, rely on four critical metrics and track them weekly: number of sales calls with decision makers, number of proposals delivered, number of signed contracts, and year-to-date revenue and margin compared to plan.

Be relentless in monitoring these metrics and even more relentless in holding your sales organization accountable for producing results. I promise you it will pay off!

The most effective organizations post sales results visibly. Post them by salesperson, and hold weekly meetings with senior management to review the sales pipeline. The objective is to know the status of every order in the pipeline.

Harris: Measures are visible and accessible to everyone: 35 percent.

One of the best ways to accomplish this is to focus on those orders with the highest probability of closing. Don't clutter the pipeline with opportunities that have a low probability of success. To differentiate between the two, use standards for assigning probabilities so that the entire sales organization speaks the same language and applies the same rules. Without standards, people apply different definitions to the selling stages and the probability of winning. And using different standards contributes to inaccurate forecasting and, ultimately, missing the top line.

The Probability of Winning Tool is one of the forty tools I use in the seminars run by The Prosen Center for Business Advancement. You can use this worksheet to improve the accuracy of your sales forecasts. Before an opportunity can be included in any sales forecast, the salesperson must assign a probability-of-winning percentage. For example, if an opportunity is assigned a 90 percent probability of winning, by definition that means all of the preceding stages have been accomplished.

Probability of Winning Tool

Stage	PW	Activities
Stage 1: Future Client Identified	**PW 10%**	• Made contact • Several conversations with decision maker • Budget owner identified • Face-to-face meetings • Need for product/service identified • Summary letter sent to document discussions and business need
Stage 2: Qualify	**PW 30%**	• ROI methodology qualified • Competition known and predisposition identified • Identify incumbent relationships • Open conversation, calls returned • Budget and need reconfirmed • Internal organization informed • Identified possible reasons for loss • Value proposition discussed
Stage 3: Validate	**PW 50%**	• Create/validate sense of urgency • Product/service trial discussed/scheduled • All influencers met • Buyer satisfied with functionality/capability • Trial close, verbal commitment • Approval path confirmed • Schedule presentation • Project approved internally
Stage 4: Presentation	**PW 70%**	• Deliver presentation • ROI methodology approved • Signature path confirmed • Timetable for signature established • Impeding events identified • All technical issues resolved • Start date confirmed
Stage 5: Pending Client Signature	**PW 90%**	• Submit paperwork • Verify all legal issues resolved • Verify everything • Are competitors still involved? • Listen for inconsistencies
Stage 6: Won	**PW 100%**	• Executed contract received • Appropriate paperwork submitted • Complete win/loss • Transition to delivery • Obtain quality introductions/referrals

(PW=probability of winning)

Not only does assigning a probability increase the reliability of your forecast, but it also ensures that everyone in sales applies the same criteria to their opportunities. If for some reason an opportunity is lost, now you have an effective method for determining why and eliminating the root cause going forward.

You also don't want sales opportunities continuously slipping from week to week. The best way to avoid this is to hold weekly pipeline review meetings. At these meetings, capture action items and use the Probability of Winning Tool to forecast revenue. These meetings should be laser-focused on what must be done to close business. They are not about listening to rationalization.

The prime way to establish an effective quota and revenue plan—and determine exactly what the target goals should be—is to secure complete buy-in from the sales leadership. Leadership should be closely involved to achieve the following goals:

- Establish stretch goals that are attainable.
- Overassign quotas to increase the probability of meeting or exceeding the plan.
- Determine the specific resources required to meet quotas and secure the associated commitments from other divisions or departments of the company.
- Develop tactical selling plans that target specific client decision makers and the reasons why they will buy.
- Have sales leaders identify any roadblocks to achieving quota and agree up front which ones to remove or reduce. It is the responsibility of the sales team to sell around those roadblocks that can't be eliminated.
- Identify specific products and services that customers want and estimate sales volume by customer, market segment, and geographic location.

Don't miss your first-quarter sales plan. Far too many companies project next year's revenue off of fourth-quarter volumes without taking into account holidays, February being a short month, and the impact of winter weather. Once you fall behind, it's very hard to recover.

Finally, if the sales organization proposes a hockey-stick forecast for meeting quota, beware! Expecting most of the sales to occur toward the end of the year seldom works. Instead, ask what it will take to achieve higher sales volumes sooner, and then ensure that the sales organization gets what it needs to succeed.

Reward Your Winners

Even when economic times are bad and businesses are under extreme pressure to contain costs, it's important to maintain a recognition and reward program to hold onto the best salespeople. That's because it's impossible to achieve bottom-line profitability solely by controlling costs. You have to grow. And to grow you have to keep your best salespeople and reward them handsomely.

Reward systems are heavily debated, but the systems that work best allow great salespeople to earn a lot of money. There should not be a cap on sales compensation, period. Design compensation systems that stimulate both margin and revenue growth so a salesperson's earnings are virtually unlimited. Once quota is achieved, continue to provide strong incentives for the remainder of the planning year. You want to design a win-win compensation system that rewards salespeople based on their ability to generate profitable new business, not live exclusively off of existing contracts and relationships. A well-designed system allows the sales team and the company to thrive.

At Sabre I was responsible for the Americas region, which represented more than half of the division's business. I asked the president what he thought about implementing a commission plan. This division of Sabre didn't have one at the time, and I thought we had to establish a commission plan to achieve and exceed our profitability goals. The president gave me the go-ahead, yet I still had one question: would he remain supportive if the plan I designed allowed someone several levels below him to make more money than he did? He was very willing. Many members of top management have trouble with this concept.

Salespeople who continue to meet and exceed their quota should be able to earn as much as possible. Remember, all good salespeople immediately decode the compensation plan to determine how to max out. If they see unlimited earnings potential, their motivation will extend beyond quotas and plans. Yes, it's expensive, but what a return on investment!

Exceeding the sales commission budget is a good problem to have when margins are maintained and profitability goals are met. The more effective the sales team is, the more profitable the company becomes, which in turn increases the valuation of the company. It's a win-win proposition for the company, its shareholders, owners, salespeople, and executives.

I have never understood why some companies still struggle with understanding this truth. Most leaders agree that compensating salespeople based on margins is the right thing to do, yet many don't do it because they can't calculate those margins. Don't let this prevent you from increasing your company's bottom line.

One more word of caution regarding compensation plans: regardless of the type of plan, salespeople will take full advantage of any loopholes and attempt to exploit the system. One of the best ways to manage this is to administer the plan from outside the sales department and closely monitor payouts to ensure profitability goals are achieved.

When I worked with Hitachi and NCR, I watched salespeople receive large bonus checks each year. It wasn't uncommon for top performers to earn high-six-figure commissions. The bonus checks brought great celebration and motivated salespeople at lower levels to work even harder.

Why? Because successful salespeople are primarily motivated by money. Beyond money, this personality type also loves public recognition. Center stage is their favorite place to be. That's why many companies tie trips and awards ceremonies to the incentive structure. Remember, these are the people who most often represent the company externally. Keep them happy and motivated, and keep the good ones on your team. You don't want them to go to your competition.

I'm often asked if it's better to hire people with strong product and service experience and teach them how to sell, or hire people with proven sales ability and teach them the company's products and services. I strongly recommend hiring people with proven sales experience in your industry or an adjacent industry. The next-best alternative is to hire people who know how to sell and teach them your products and services. It's far too difficult to teach people how to sell, and it rarely works.

Communicate Your Expectations

If price weren't an issue, anyone could sell. Selling value, however, is a much different proposition. To sell value, a salesperson must ask the right questions and know when to be quiet. Your salesperson needs to be incredibly well versed in the competitive landscape and understand the customer's business. Great salespeople know the importance of developing strong client relationships. Ultimately these relationships lead to customer loyalty and increasing customer share. The sales organization sets the tone for establishing these relationships.

To ensure the groundwork is laid to create customers for life, management must communicate the following to the sales organization:

- Present the company's value proposition and be able to differentiate and sell value.

- Focus on selling the company's existing products and services and minimize "one-offs."
- Sell to target customers and markets.
- Avoid being a stalking horse—only go after business you can win.
- Provide accurate and timely sales data to the company's sales force automation (SFA) and customer relationship management (CRM) systems.
- Be a careful listener and ask insightful questions to gain information and build credibility.
- Determine customer needs and directly address them.
- Know your client's budgeting and buying cycle.
- Know the competition.
- Underpromise and overdeliver.
- Never commit to anything the company can't deliver: dates, services, terms, or scope.
- Include a detailed scope of work and specific customer success criteria to avoid any misunderstandings.
- Follow the company's contract approval process.
- Involve the delivery organization in complicated sales to properly set customer expectations before contract signing.
- Involve senior management to help close important new business.
- Become expert at handling objections.
- Know when to be silent.
- Know how to close and ask for the sale.
- Recruit great salespeople; don't teach great people how to sell.

I was recently asked to work with two veteran private-client financial advisors at Merrill Lynch to help them close two important accounts they had been working on for more than a year. Using the tools and tactics from my workshop, we spent two hours role-playing and coaching. Shortly thereafter, they won both accounts.

To increase sales, try using the following vernacular*:

LANGUAGE TO USE	LANGUAGE TO AVOID
Presentation	Pitch
Investment	Price/Cost
Own	Buy
Future Client	Prospect
Companies We Serve	Customer
Agreement	Contract
Approve	Sign

Support Sales with Essential Business Processes

The company must back up every step of the sales process at the same time these sales-improvement techniques are implemented. Management must ensure that the sales team never has to worry about the company's ability to deliver on its promises. Salespeople are responsible for selling, and should not be burdened with other internal functions. If they are, the top line will suffer. To support the sales organization, management must provide systems and tools, and establish internal processes that provide the following:

- Accurate sales forecasting and pipeline management
- Clear definitions of all selling stages and win probabilities
- Contracts with clear terms dealing with business disputes, payment terms, discounts, renewals, etc.
- A documented contract approval process that is clearly communicated and accurately followed

* Tom Hopkins International, *Boot Camp Sales Mastery*, 2003

- Financial and legal review of contracts and proposals before customer signature to minimize contractual penalties whenever possible
- Replication of top sales successes and a process to share lessons learned
- Capture of customer feedback to enhance revenue opportunities
- Senior management to help close important new business
- The elimination of delivery or support problems that impede sales
- A defined process that quickly provides a go/no-go decision to one-off opportunities

The Role of Sales in Public and Government Organizations

In public entities such as local school districts and local government organizations, marketing replaces the traditional role of sales. Funding for public schools is from tax revenue and government programs. The best way to increase funding is to provide high-quality education measured by high completion rates and test scores. Schools capable of achieving these outcomes are in a strong position to retain and attract more students and associated tax revenue.

City governments also are funded from local tax revenue and have to provide quality services and promote themselves to attract and retain new residents and businesses. Some cities may also find additional sources of revenue by providing services such as fleet maintenance to other local agencies. In this environment, marketing and new business development are essential to maintain and grow revenue.

Maximize the Value of Marketing

Marketing can provide great value to a sales organization and the company's bottom line if programs are directly correlated to generating new sales and profitability. However, to ensure this, you must hold marketing leaders accountable for measurable results and audit programs to verify outcomes. Marketing must understand and communicate in the language of business leaders. This includes knowing how their programs impact earnings, cash flow, return on investment (ROI), and net present value (NPV). If not, marketing will be underutilized and viewed strictly as a discretionary expense that is continuously targeted for budget cuts.

To provide direct and meaningful value to the sales organization, marketing must achieve the following:

- Create the intersection of the company's products and services with customers who will buy them.
- Provide insightful, real-time, competitive information to help win more sales.
- Focus on supporting products and services based on verifiable customer demand.
- Know what's selling, what isn't, and why—and then adjust accordingly. Find this out by asking structured questions of salespeople and current customers, and by using focus groups.
- Include input from the sales organization early in new product studies to ensure that customers have a real need for the product and are willing to pay an appropriate price.
- Travel with the sales force to better understand customer requirements.
- Become the sales organization's best friend by helping to increase sales.
- Take responsibility for producing measurable bottom-line results.

Most companies lack sufficient information about their competitors and a process for collecting, maintaining, and sharing that information. Here are several sources for obtaining competitive intelligence:

- Dun and Bradstreet
- Hoover's
- The Internet
- Industry Conferences
- Your competitors' in-person and online seminars, plus any information an employee is willing to give over the phone
- Potential customers, especially those who are dissatisfied with your competition
- Your competitors' best salespeople (once you've hired them)
- Technical people working for your competitors—most of them like to talk about their company
- Sales literature from your competitors

Does Your Sales Team Measure Up?

Ask these key questions—each should be answered with a resounding *yes!* Here are six of the most important criteria you can use to evaluate your sales effectiveness.

Does my sales team

1. Consistently meet or exceed revenue and margin goals?
2. Focus on selling the company's existing products and services and minimize one-offs?
3. Enter accurate and timely sales data into the company's SFA/CRM systems?
4. Know the competition in-depth and how to differentiate our company and its products and/or services from others?

5. Involve senior management to help close important new business?
6. Only pursue the business they can win?

Very Important Lessons

Over the years, working with many different companies, I have learned the following actions ultimately make sales effectiveness a strong contributor to achieving and accelerating profitability:

- Listen very carefully. Understand what the sales force is saying to ensure that the right actions are taken to increase revenue.
- Focus on results rather than rationalization. Selling is all about the numbers.
- Remove roadblocks and remain focused on results, not excuses.
- Get quota buy-in from sales management, and hold management accountable for producing results.
- React quickly if revenue falls behind plan. It's very difficult to get caught up.
- Visibly post results.
- Replicate success.
- Exceed the commission budget when quota is tied to margin.
- Cut scope instead of price.
- Have financial and legal departments review contracts before customer approval.
- Do whatever it takes, ethically, to get customers to like you, trust you, listen to you, and buy from you.
- Be a focused questioner, an active listener, and a closer, and make sure your salespeople are as well.

ACTIONS TO TAKE NOW

Write down actions to take now for the following questions:

1. How can you recruit great salespeople instead of teaching people how to sell?
2. Are you satisfied with the accuracy of your sales forecast? If not, establish clear win-probability criteria and standard definitions for all selling stages.
3. Do you know at a moment's notice what closed today? How can you be sure that you will always be aware of this information?
4. Do you have salespeople behind quota? If so, for how long, and what will be done to correct the situation?
5. If you have results that are falling behind plan, list what corrective actions you will take, when you will take them, and whom you will involve.

Now that you know much more about sales effectiveness and are acting to maximize it, please turn your attention to a third attribute of highly profitable companies—operational excellence. Once a sale is made, a company's ability to operate efficiently determines whether margins are made or lost.

FOUR

Operational Excellence: The Secret Formula for Extraordinary Results

A thorough understanding of a company's cost structure and the use of continuous process improvement provide the foundation for many business decisions. Without accurate cost information it's impossible to set optimal prices, forecast performance, isolate areas that negatively impact cash flow, determine what to stop doing, identify what to automate, and decide how best to manage costs. It's also critical to understand cost drivers in order to grow a profitable business while investing in areas that improve profitability and de-investing in ones that don't.

Operational excellence is how margins are maintained. It is about efficiency, effectiveness, and doing the right things right the first time. As discussed in the previous chapter, sales are essential to profitability because they fuel business growth. However, when sales fall short of the top line, or there is pricing pressure, most companies must cut costs to maintain margins and stay afloat. Unfortunately that often means eliminating people. It's best to keep a constant eye on costs instead of slashing payroll as a last-ditch effort to make ends meet.

Managing cost is a balancing act. To carefully maintain margins and help avoid reactive cost cutting, all costs must be explicitly tied to the business plan. This enables you to modify costs in a disciplined and well-planned manner as the company accelerates or decelerates.

In a recent business effectiveness study conducted by The Prosen Center for Business Advancement, top executives of more than sixty companies and organizations rated themselves and their enterprises on their level of operational effectiveness. Findings revealed the following strengths and weaknesses:

Strengths

- We have a well-defined cost structure that is understood throughout management: 69 percent.
- I receive accurate and timely cost reports that promote effective decision making: 61 percent.

Weaknesses

- We have a defined process for eliminating inefficiencies: 19 percent.
- We effectively manage employee productivity: 31 percent.
- We have a deep understanding of our competitors' cost structure and respond quickly to changes: 32 percent.

Where do you and your company fit within these strengths and weaknesses? How would you rate yourself? How would you rate your organization?

Know Your Cost Structure

The first step toward operational excellence is to thoroughly understand your company's cost structure. This provides the foundation for sound business decisions across the entire company. Without accurate cost information, it's impossible to set proper prices, forecast performance, isolate areas that negatively impact cash flow, or determine what to stop doing, what to automate, how to allocate funds, or how best to manage budgets. It's also critical to understand cost drivers in order to grow a profitable business while investing in areas to improve profitability and results while de-investing in ones that don't.

At NCR, I had the opportunity to work for Mark Hurd, who was recently named chief executive officer and president of Hewlett-Packard. Mark is one of the best at improving operating efficiency. While working for him, I admired his ability to cut to the chase, make sense out of data, and take action to improve the company's financial performance. Under his leadership, NCR's revenue, earnings, and stock price dramatically improved. All too often leaders become slaves to their financial accounting systems and wait too long before taking action. If you don't completely understand your cost structure, you're at a competitive disadvantage. Take whatever steps are necessary to get the information you need. There is no excuse for not knowing.

It's amazing how many companies struggle to accurately determine their true cost of doing business (the cost of labor; fixed and variable costs; direct and indirect expenses; overhead; costs by market segment, customer, geography, or product). Clear cost accounting allows a company to focus its energies on winning in the marketplace and achieving its objectives instead of debating the numbers internally.

Management's primary objective in operational excellence is to fully understand all costs of doing business and maintain the proper balance of cost in relation to revenue. That's the best way to ensure that you maintain margins. If you are in a commodity-based business, you must be a low-cost producer. If you sell differentiation, your prices must support a higher cost structure. It's that simple! The goal is not across-the-board cost minimization, but rather optimization in support of achieving your business objectives.

For public entities such as schools and local governments, the objectives are to accurately understand all the costs of running the organization and to ensure budgets are properly allocated and funds are used efficiently to achieve the organization's top objectives. Operational excellence is a vital element since these organizations operate primarily on fixed budgets, with little opportunity to increase funding.

However, if you don't understand and track your costs in sufficient detail, it's impossible to know where to make the necessary adjustments to improve profitability. This is not the place to be guessing; the risk is too great. Devote resources to determining not only your own but also your competitors' cost structure.

When you grow your company, you grow your cost structure. You want to make sure you're growing it in the right proportion to revenue by adding cost only in areas where revenue is increasing and where margins and profitability can be maintained or improved.

Strategic investments are viewed differently from other types of costs. These investments must be made using strict justification and approval guidelines. Every department should use the same approach to enable effective comparison and selection of the appropriate investment alternatives. These standards include use of approved financial justification methods such as NPV, ROI, EVA (economic value added), and payback, approved hurdle rates, proper depreciation schedules, and approved investment categories. Tight-spending authorities are required to maintain control over the total cost of investments and minimize contingent expenditures. In addition, post-investment audits at the conclusion of a project are essential to help managers make better future investment decisions. In all cases, managers should be held accountable for investment outcomes.

The cost candidates that *should* be considered for growth include production and delivery costs, sales, customer service, and product support. The latter two cost categories should only grow in support of the company's service strategy. These costs are all directly attributable to revenue increases. Realize that to increase profitability you either have to increase prices or only allow these costs to grow in decreasing proportion to revenue. Manage costs tightly. They shouldn't grow unless some predetermined efficiency standards are met. That includes all overhead cost areas, such as human resources, accounting, administrative, and support costs.

If not closely managed, these costs mysteriously grow by one person or investment at a time until they represent a significant and unnecessary burden on the business. In lieu of increasing these costs, look for alternatives; for instance, outsourcing functions such as recruiting, training development, payroll, and copy reproduction. Deploy technology such as PDAs to allow employees to manage their own schedules, and e-mail and follow up on calls without administrative support. Automate expense reporting, document approval processes, and benefits administration. Use the tools discussed later in this chapter to reduce rework and redundancies such as billing errors and warranty claims.

Often, companies increase overhead because, for example, line organizations are not getting effective centralized corporate support, and therefore the company adds their own local support resources. You must not allow this to happen.

One way to minimize incremental overhead costs is to develop an approval process where *every* requested increase receives senior management's attention. It's not okay to allow these costs to grow just because the company is meeting its profitability objectives. This may sound burdensome. However, it's far better to take the time to think through these decisions when times are good than be forced to take draconian actions when tough times arrive.

Always run lean, particularly when your company is doing well. That's the perfect time to increase cash reserves and invest in the future. Get into the habit. The dividends are great.

Invest in Your Accounting System

To understand your costs—accurately and in real-time—you have to invest in your financial accounting systems. I can't tell you how often I've worked with companies that don't know their cost of doing business in sufficient detail to support their business decisions. It's as bad as driving your car using only the rearview mirror. It's just a matter of time before you'll crash.

The market will change. With an accounting system tailored to your business, you can immediately adjust costs with confidence and remain competitive. When your business grows your costs will naturally increase. An accurate financial accounting system will enable you to scale your growth, increasing margins with revenue. Without effective financial systems, you can't compare your budget, assumptions, and plans with actual results at a level discrete enough to make effective decisions.

Why guess when you can know? Remember, it's a lot harder to cut expenses than to grow efficiently.

I once worked with a Fortune 1000 company that didn't have a detailed accounting system to determine which products, projects, customers, markets, or regions were profitable. As a result, it was impossible to hold anyone accountable for financial results. What I soon found out was that I had inherited a company division that was losing $9 million a year, and no one knew it! By applying the tools and tactics in this book, we turned a yearly loss of 30 percent into a gain of 21 percent in twelve months.

One of the first changes we made was to establish an accounting system that enabled us to make decisions based on fact and to hold decision makers accountable. This new financial management system required the business culture to change. Various divisions had to share data that had once been very closely held. Eventually, despite the $9 million deficit, we were able to achieve the highest sales and profit margins in the division.

We accomplished this by first fully understanding our cost structure. Then we invested in both people and systems to establish the information and processes that we needed to stay in control.

Often clients tell me they can't afford to make these investments. What they are really saying is that it's not important to them to know how well their business is performing. Yet the required information can often be obtained with a minimal investment in an off-the-shelf software package or using existing systems with minor modifications and the help of a skilled report writer.

For example, while helping City Sprint, a leading courier company in Dallas, I introduced the owners to an expert systems administrator. He was able to extract critical data from disparate systems and automate key reports. These changes gave the owners a better understanding of their business and enabled them to make better decisions.

Get Close to Your Cost Drivers

It's also critical to understand exactly what drives cost so you know how to profitably grow your business. Budgets must have clearly defined assumptions pertaining to cost drivers, which lead to better decisions on how to protect profitability against variations in revenue and pricing. This is the only way to accurately invest in areas that improve profitability and de-invest in ones that don't.

For example, as revenues increase, there should be a preapproved cost model that allows specific costs to change according to established efficiency standards. These efficiency standards allow companies to scale up and operate at optimal capacity that achieves maximum margins. This means you have to know how much work your people and systems can handle before you make incremental investments.

To accomplish this, you must measure productivity and have documented plans that include time frames for investing in efficiency-improving technologies when certain predetermined thresholds are met.

Searching for new ways to do more with less is a never-ending process. To measure productivity requires time and activity reporting. This is a rich source of information if it is used effectively.

To get the most from your time-reporting system, follow these simple rules:

- Design the system with a minimum number of accounting categories.
- Avoid using a catchall category like "other." Time reported as "other" isn't specific enough to aid decision making.
- Train everyone on how to use the system.
- Most importantly, enforce reporting requirements or people will not comply.

Knowing how people spend their time will help you prioritize potential areas for cost reduction and automation. Here are some of the reporting categories you should capture, trend, and compare to budget:

- Administration (e.g., e-mail and paperwork)
- Training
- Internal meetings
- Internal systems support

- Vacation
- Sick time
- Customer support
- Production
- Product support
- Product development
- Documentation
- Project management

Categories such as customer support can be further broken down:

- Collection of accounts receivable
- Problem resolution
- Billing adjustments
- Warranty work

Cost categories will vary by department and company, based on the type of work being performed. What's important is to get started. Begin by selecting appropriate time-reporting categories, start capturing employees' time, and track results. You might be amazed at what you find, and more importantly, what you can do to increase efficiency.

Assign Every Cost an Owner

With effective financial accounting systems, leaders have ready access to accurate information and can be held accountable for financial results. A clear financial-reporting process, coupled with assigned ownership, will help companies avoid wasting time in endless debate.

Let's start with overhead, which is one of the most hotly contested costs of doing business. It's imperative to establish a process that enables you to accurately account for and manage these costs. This is an area that often generates heated debate, and without a tightly managed process, gamesmanship can lead to inferior decision making.

Some overhead is required to run a business. The real issue is how these costs are distributed, managed, and approved. Once the allocation model is developed, it's imperative that all senior management and P&L holders understand and buy into the process. Do not allow managers to exploit the system to improve their financial results. All overhead costs must be covered. It's just that simple.

I once worked for a company where exploiting the system was viewed as a sport. For example, one department decided to allow their staff to telecommute in order to argue against any corporate allocation of floor space and facilities. We wasted many hours debating this issue, knowing all along these fixed costs had to be fully recovered whether employees worked on-site or at home.

Few people want more than their fair share of overhead, and the best way to address this is by following a defined process that clearly outlines the approval process for allocating and increasing overhead. A similar process must also be in place to manage all noncorporate overhead. Overhead costs must directly contribute to accomplishing the company's top objectives. If they don't, eliminate them. For this process to work, there can be no entitlement policies or sacred cows.

Marketing is often mistaken for an unnecessary cost. When times are great, resources are devoted to marketing. But when times are tough, marketing is usually one of the first areas cut. This action is shortsighted, because marketing can be a primary sales driver. Marketing professionals must be able to articulate their department's value in bottom-line results. Marketing leaders need to evaluate their programs in terms of return on investment and be accountable for results. This accountability enables marketing to be considered a required investment, not a discretionary expense. Once again, it pays off to have people in place who know how to produce tangible results.

When it comes to budgeting and results reporting, hold functional leaders or managers—not the financial staff—accountable for the creation and execution of budgets and plans. During budget review, leaders are required to know the details and to explain all deviations from the plan along with developing and implementing specific actions to achieve the plan. After all, explanations don't win—results do.

Another important and often overlooked aspect of operational excellence is regularly comparing actual costs to budget assumptions—not just the numbers in the plan. Understanding assumption deviations will help improve the accuracy of future forecasting.

With a full understanding of your cost structure and the marketplace, effective cost management will help you make profitable decisions. If a division wants to hire new personnel, for instance, you should determine what each person would cost. If profitability and attainment of the company's top objectives won't be directly impacted by adding the person, then your decision is simple: don't hire. If help is needed to get through a well-defined, critical situation, consider using contract resources for a specific, short period of time. Every cost must be justified by its potential to increase profitability.

I once worked for a company that applied zero-based budgeting across the board to regain cost control. No one liked it because we had to start at zero with each budget year and justify every penny we wanted to spend. It required us to analyze every spending area and cut what wasn't needed. As a result, we utilized resources much more efficiently. This was a painful but effective way to turn around a company that had been running in the red. Consider using this technique when dealing with specific trouble spots.

When costs are not constantly measured against revenue, profit will be endangered. Companies that move fast to address cost issues and don't rationalize their cost structure maintain profitability. After all, when costs are out of control they rarely get better on their own. Instead, they often grow worse. Running leaner rather than letting costs slowly creep out of control is the best way to grow your company profitably.

Another great way to reduce costs is to periodically challenge why every report in your company is required. If you do this effectively and don't accept rationalization, you will find many opportunities to save money by halting unproductive activity. I applied this seemingly simple strategy inside a Fortune 1000 company and the savings was extraordinary. The company devoted people and systems to generating volumes of reports that no one used or even understood the reasons for producing. Often, the simplest actions make a real difference.

Since the late 1990s, U.S. companies have experienced several waves of major layoffs. While many blamed the stock market, the major culprit was lack of operational excellence. As companies grew in the late 1990s, 2000, and 2001, they expanded at any cost. They hired people regardless of real need. When the top line was not achieved, overhead costs were fixed at a level impossible to maintain. As a result, people were cut.

If you grow a company and only add essential costs, when growth slows overhead will be more manageable. As a result, you will have the resources to solve problems and succeed, while competitors who have laid off employees will suffer a severe loss of human capital that is often essential to regain profitability.

Move Swiftly, Watch Every Turn

Operational excellence allows you to quickly zero in on problem areas. When costs escalate, profitability will be affected. Immediate action will be required to correct the situation, or it will most likely worsen.

Poor quality and resulting rework can quickly increase a company's cost structure and render it noncompetitive. With all the investments made in quality processes over the years, you would think this issue would be very well managed. Yet when I ask company leaders how many of them have defined processes in place to reduce inefficiencies and rework, very few do. This is validated in the business effectiveness study results at the beginning of the chapter. I believe the major reason for this is that leaders don't know which tools to use or how to use them to get results without getting bogged down in the process.

One of the most effective ways to reduce unnecessary cost is to have a robust quality process that utilizes root-cause analysis (RCA) and irreversible corrective action (ICA). These techniques ensure the company removes inefficiencies and reduces rework by doing the right thing right the first time.

RCA and ICA are the two most important principles you need to know to help reduce unnecessary costs while increasing product and service quality. RCA in its simplest form means being able to determine the root cause of problems and inefficiencies instead of dealing with symptoms. For example, the symptom associated with a customer complaint might be that the delivery date was missed. The root cause was a product shortage that the purchasing department knew about and failed to either obtain approval for expedite charges or give advance notice to the customer.

By addressing the symptom, you will apologize to the customer and possibly issue some form of credit, leaving yourself open for the same problem to happen again. However, if you identify the root cause and implement ICA by training the purchasing department, you will prevent the same problem from recurring. You also will improve customer satisfaction and avoid unnecessary costs going forward. ICA ensures that the root causes of problems are resolved so they never occur again. This is a very high standard to maintain, but well worth the investment.

The following is an example of how to apply RCA and ICA to an accounts-receivable business problem.

STEP 1: Identify the problem. The problem must be quantifiable and measurable.

- The percentage of accounts receivable more than ninety days old has exceeded the company goal of 5 percent.

STEP 2: Determine the most likely cause categories.

- Invoices not received by customers
- Billing disputes
- Invoice-approval delays
- Special terms extended
- Pending legal and collection action

STEP 3: Collect data.

- Log every invoice that goes from the eighty-ninth day to the ninetieth day by cause category for one month and calculate the percentage each cause category represents of the total.

STEP 4: Represent the data.

- Using bar charts, graph four weeks of data by cause category to determine trends and volume.

STEP 5: Create a Pareto diagram.

- Create a Pareto diagram to determine which cause categories represent greater than 80 percent of the problem. The objective is to avoid spending time on the less important cause categories.

Here is an example of an accounts receivable Pareto diagram that is used to determine the categories responsible for 80 percent of a receivables problem. Having this information presented visually helps you to focus resources on the areas causing most of the problems. For example, billing disputes combined with invoice approval delays represent 85.3 percent of the receivables problem. Without this information, it's easy to spend valuable resources on less important issues, such as special terms, which represent less than 4 percent of the problem.

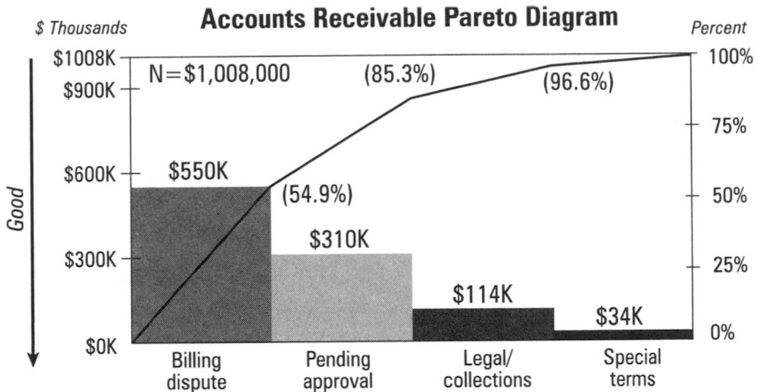

The Pareto diagram is another of the forty tools I teach in the workshops run by The Prosen Center for Business Advancement.

STEP 6: Determine RCA for billing disputes identified in Step 5.

- Inaccurate time charged to jobs
- Working with the wrong client contacts to approve invoices

STEP 7: Implement ICA test.

- Train a subset of workers on correct use of the time-reporting procedures and monitor adherence.
- Change the process to provide a subset of customer service representatives with updated customer contact lists and training.

STEP 8: Track results for three weeks to validate improvement.

STEP 9: Institutionalize ICA.

- Train the entire department, document the process, and track ongoing metrics to ensure gains are maintained.

STEP 10: Repetition.

- Repeat Steps 5–9 with the next largest cause category ("pending approval" in the example), until the company is once again achieving its accounts receivable goals.

The last company I ran experienced a number of network failures that denied customers access to their vital systems. When this happened, it was so easy to pat ourselves on the back after restoring service in record time. Instead of a two-hour outage, we had a one-hour outage. Yet from the customer's perspective, the time differential meant nothing. The customer didn't want an outage in the first place!

So we started to look at what caused that problem. Was it hardware? What specific component failed? Was it a procedure that didn't work? Or was it a training problem? This process took time, yet it was important to know why—to get to the root cause instead of dealing with symptoms—and to eventually improve customer satisfaction and reduce our cost structure. In the end we stopped the problems from recurring, and we soon led the industry in network availability. The root cause was a combination of ineffective change-management procedures and inferior network architecture. ICA involved documenting processes, training, and installing some additional hardware.

Another time, after closely reviewing time reports, we found an underutilized group of highly skilled technicians tucked away inside the operations department. Because of a lack of proper accountability their sole job was to relay and follow up on trouble reports between customer service and the repair technicians. This inefficient process created incredibly high people costs. And the people in those positions felt frustrated and miserable because they knew the process was broken, yet they were being used to address the symptoms instead of the root cause.

I met with the employees to verify the findings and to deploy them to other positions in the company where they could fully utilize their skills and perform valuable functions. We solved this issue by changing the process. Customers' problems were then put directly in the hands of the people responsible for solving the problems.

Here is the key: The productivity reports yielded the first clue that we were having a problem. From there I held skip-level meetings with the people responsible for doing the work to validate the problem, get their input, change the process, and reassign the resources.

Eventually we ran the entire company using these problem-solving techniques. Once we had enough results to back up our success, we were able to bring existing and future customers into the business and show them the error-removal processes we used that translated into more sales, better service, and, ultimately, higher customer loyalty. Of course, this improved process also had a profound impact on the bottom line. Making continuous process improvement and zero defects the standard instead of the exception has allowed companies such as FedEx to differentiate themselves and dominate the market.

Another great way to focus on problem elimination is to hold recurring operations reviews. The process I like best makes the leader who is responsible for each operating area stand up and present his or her results in front of colleagues and senior management. The key to these reviews is the use of trend charts that show results week-to-week or month-to-month compared to plan. The objective is to improve results by reducing the number of problem occurrences. Conversation during these reviews should focus solely on how RCA and ICA are being used to accomplish this goal. Let the numbers do the talking. You'd be surprised what they reveal about the organization's level of understanding and accountability.

Here are some areas in business that benefit greatly from RCA and ICA analysis:

- Customer service calls
- Billing errors
- Accounts receivable
- Warranty claims
- Returns
- Refunds and credits
- Spoilage
- Waste
- Customer churn
- Win/loss reviews
- Employee turnover
- On-the-job accidents
- Information system performance

Commit yourself and your organization to RCA and ICA and watch your profitability, productivity, and customer service improve.

Does Your Operational Excellence Measure Up?

To help companies evaluate their own operational excellence, I ask key questions that should each be answered with a resounding *yes!* Here are four of the most important criteria you can use to evaluate your operational excellence.

Do we

1. Receive accurate and timely cost reports that promote effective decision making?
2. Have a deep understanding of our competitors' cost structure and respond quickly to changes?
3. Effectively manage employee productivity?
4. Have a defined process for eliminating inefficiencies?

Very Important Lessons

Over the years, working with many different companies, I have learned a number of lessons that leaders can use to make operational excellence a strong contributor to achieving and accelerating profitability:

- Run leaner than you would prefer—even in good times. It's always a better alternative to budget cuts and layoffs.
- Review budgets monthly and concentrate on any negative deviations. Replicate positive deviations.
- Don't allow costs to get out in front of revenue and profitability. Many companies have learned this lesson the hard way.
- Take swift action when budgets deviate and profitability is being challenged.
- Demand clear ownership of all costs. Owners must have decision-making authority and be held accountable for meeting cost objectives.
- Consider the value of zero-based budgeting, especially in turning around specific trouble spots.
- Just because the total expense budget is being met doesn't mean each line item is in balance. Know the details, and be careful of aggregation.
- Dump the "It's in the budget, so let's spend it" attitude.
- Just because it's being done now doesn't mean it has to continue. If something doesn't add directly to the bottom line, then stop doing it.
- Scrutinize expense reports thoroughly. Don't allow the approval process to become a formality.
- Beware of incremental pricing. All costs, not just fixed costs, must be covered.
- Develop the means to collect competitive cost information.

- Remember that everything is renegotiable: leases, vendor agreements, etc.
- Whenever possible, write your own contracts to increase the chance of setting better terms.

ACTIONS TO TAKE NOW

There are many action items and questions in this chapter, so I'll end with some of the Big Picture actions to take now.

1. Have you defined processes to eliminate inefficiency? If not, what steps will you take to accomplish this?
2. How effectively do you manage employee productivity? List three ways you can do even better.
3. How does your company know the cost structure of your competitors?
4. How accurate are your product and service margins? How do you know?

Operational excellence is essential to accelerating profitability, but all company profitability planning comes together in finance. Financial management, the fourth attribute of highly profitable companies discussed in the next chapter, is where accountability is maintained, forecasts are developed, results are measured and reported, data is transformed into information, and, ultimately, the company's financial health is determined.

FIVE

Financial Management: Where Information Is Power

Financial management represents the center of accountability within a company. This is where all planning comes together, where forecasts are developed, assumptions are challenged, results are measured and reported, and where information pertaining to the financial health of the business is communicated both internally and externally. This is also where controls are established, investments are evaluated, and audits are performed.

Finance is an often-untapped resource that should be an integral, proactive component of the leadership team rather than being limited to financial accounting and report generating. No other function can tell as much about a company's financial health. This chapter is not focused on legal reporting requirements, standard financial ratios, or accounting methods. The focus, instead, is on what highly profitable companies require from their finance team to remain in control, achieve their goals, and stay ahead of the competition. To accomplish this leaders must shift their thinking to give finance the authority to take on this important role within the company.

On more than one occasion, I've overheard people in finance say, "I wish they would ask me what's going on and what should be done to improve results. Instead, they just expect me to produce reports."

Finance is key to profitability because it touches all parts of the business: employees, customers, and shareholders. The finance department manages accounts payable, receivables, and billing, thereby representing the company externally every bit as much as sales or customer service. And in public companies, finance also represents the business to investors and the financial community. Finance is about perspective—providing context for decisions, holistic solutions, alternatives, and ideas for positive change. Finance also focuses on control and provides companies with the required checks and balances to understand and manage their fiscal performance.

One of the companies I was brought in to lead was making the top line, but their margins were shrinking. I asked our finance team to determine the source of the problem and develop specific recommendations to restore margins. This wasn't the usual way of solving problems. Traditionally, the executive team studied various data sources and reports in order to determine the cause of a problem, and then told people how to solve it. I was not satisfied with that approach and decided to tap into the people who I thought knew the most—finance.

Within a couple of days, we had our answer. The problem was that we were selling the wrong product mix. The products with smaller margins were being sold to make quota. The solution recommended by finance was to change the sales incentive plan to encourage the sale of the higher-margin products. It worked!

Sounds simple, doesn't it? You would be surprised at how many companies overlook the obvious and spend too much time chasing problems that don't exist.

For example, one of the surveys done by The Prosen Center for Business Advancement determined that 64 percent of respondents said financial management took a leadership role in the business-planning process. Only 39 percent of these most senior executives, however, said that financial management provided "early-warning" information by tracking key leading indicators to help anticipate change and minimize surprises in the business environment.

You can do better by following the key financial management functions that keep highly profitable companies in the black. This section shows you how to turn data into information and how to unlock the hidden intelligence of your financial organization to enhance decision making.

Anticipate Every Turn

The primary objective of effective financial management is to keep the company focused on achieving profitability objectives with minimal surprises along the way. Financial management drives the company's economic engine by continually recommending financial enhancements and using a deep understanding of the business to assist in decision making. Yet to be truly effective, the financial management team must be proactive and provide insightful input directly to top decision makers.

It's important to differentiate financial management from cost management. Cost management is primarily an inwardly focused analysis that requires an understanding of what's going on inside the company to ensure that required margins are maintained. Financial management involves looking both inside and outside the company to calculate the influence of external factors on the business. Your financial management team must not only understand the inner workings of the business, but also have the financial expertise to prepare and understand the numbers, translate them into information, and offer insightful recommendations to help leaders achieve the company's ultimate agenda—financial success.

The financial management team must understand both finance and the business. This is a tall order for most companies. It's hard to find people who have deep knowledge in both areas. I remember searching for months to find the right person, and when I did, I brought him with me whenever I changed companies. The person I'm referring to is Lambert Mathieu. Shortly after joining Sabre, I determined stronger financial support was required to improve our performance. I set out to find the most talented financial leader within the company and was fortunate to meet Lambert. I knew immediately he was the right person for the job. Lambert knew the company, the systems, the people, what needed to be changed, and, more importantly, he wasn't afraid to speak up. Lambert, along with James Pinckney, Brian Carpenter, Ken Pedersen, and other members of my leadership team successfully turned a business's 30 percent loss into a 21 percent gain in just over twelve months.

Finance Knows Where Profit Is Made—or Lost

Financial management is one of The Five Attributes of Highly Profitable Companies because this is where data is transformed into information that's used to make decisions. Financial management is constantly questioning where the profit is truly made in the company, which products and services are performing well, how to meet budget and program requirements, what actions are required to optimize wins and fix or eliminate losses, what capital needs are now and what they are projected to be in the future, how to position the business to best meet those capital needs, how much profit will be needed to meet future capital requirements, if profit and cash flow objectives are being met, what actions are required to improve profitability, and how to increase the accuracy of financial forecasts.

Finance must always be ahead of the game, negotiating excellent terms for the business, and constantly looking for ways to improve the balance sheet. The finance organization should never be satisfied. It should always be seeking new, innovative ways to improve the financials and create more profit or surpluses for the economic engine.

Accountability, Not Just Accounting

When companies fail to achieve their profitability goals, I often see that their finance team is concerned with accounting but not accountability. Usually I can trace a company's demise to the CFO's door. If your CFO is a follower and not a leader, your business is in jeopardy. A financial leader proactively finds problems, anticipates changes, rallies resources, articulates problems, provides information and recommendations to improve the situation, and holds the organization accountable.

A financial leader incites action sooner rather than later. Finance is the best place to see everything that's good and bad about your company's financial performance. Make certain the person in charge has the courage, expertise, and authority to lead based on this information.

One sign of an ineffective finance organization is when individual business units begin building their own "internal" finance departments because they aren't getting what they need from the finance team. If you see this develop at your company, finance is not being held accountable, and, therefore, is in no position to hold the entire company accountable. Take immediate action. Not only is finance underperforming, the additional staff is reducing your profit margins unnecessarily.

Finance Takes the Lead in Planning

Finance should not be viewed strictly as central control. This team should also play a vital role in planning to ensure that the necessary checks and balances are in place to increase the odds of achieving the company's objectives.

P&L and business-unit owners are ultimately responsible for producing the results forecasted in the business plan. However, finance should guide the processes to ensure that budgets are reasonable and linked to plan achievement. Therefore, detailed action plans, often called operational plans, must accompany budgets, showing how objectives will be achieved. Finance should constantly challenge the plan for doability and reasonability by establishing measurements to evaluate ongoing performance.

It's crucial to get buy-in from business-unit owners early in the planning process to eliminate debate and ensure that effective, useful measurements are established to track performance. Remember, it's not a debate; it's all about results.

Finance is where the business is held accountable for making money. It all starts with planning and making budget assumptions. Document, discuss, and gain P&L and business-unit owner support for all assumptions used in planning and pro forma creation. Don't approve budgets based on faith, trust, and the hope of getting lucky. Instead, challenge assumptions to ensure that they are feasible and based on sound logic.

Assumptions such as labor rates, head count, cost of goods, productivity, overhead allocation, revenue, market share, pricing, exchange rates, and product volumes must be supported before being approved. Once decisions have been made, continuously update these assumptions with current data, and regularly review them to hold each area accountable to the plan. Assumption analysis is an essential, and often overlooked, component of the budget review process, so actively involve the financial team in all budget review meetings to help enforce accountability.

Assumption analysis is also critical to understanding the reason for budget deviations. Why were results better than planned? What assumption changed, or how did you execute better than expected? You need this information to create better forecasts, replicate successes, and mitigate risk.

Finance should also be responsible for scheduling frequent budget reviews with all responsible parties. During these meetings the business-unit leaders, not finance, are responsible for explaining their performance in detail. These meetings are vital to staying on course. Therefore, top management should make proper attendance, participation, and progress priorities for everyone involved.

Finance Must Speak Your Language

If your finance team is generating reports that no one in the company understands—or needs—it's time for an overhaul. Reports should be concise, timely, accurate, meaningful, and insightful. They should also be presented in the terms the business leaders need to manage their business. To do this, finance must proactively seek out business-unit leaders, determine what they need to run their organizations, and provide them with that information.

When I speak with CEOs and other senior executives, I ask if they frequently take home stacks of financial reports to review and decipher. The answer is almost always yes. I also ask how many actually get through all the information without falling asleep. I think you know the answer.

I was in the same position for many years until I developed a one-page report that gave me all the information I needed to understand the performance of *any* size company. This tool is designed specifically to help managers and leaders simplify and identify the information that matters most.

Finance should also provide timely information and real-time data analysis, so you can act immediately. Therefore, invest in systems that enable you to quickly recognize and capitalize on changing situations. It's impossible to effectively run a business with information thirty, sixty, or in some instances ninety days behind month-end close.

If your company has this problem, implement a financial accounting process that provides you the information you need when you need it. Otherwise you will be reacting to the past while your competition is planning for the future.

Some organizations make things happen, some watch things happen, and others ask what the heck just happened. Leave the last two situations for your competitors.

Results reporting is not rocket science. An easy way to represent results is by a simple trend analysis that compares actual results over time to the business plan and clearly shows deviations. Use color-coded, quick-read visuals. Red means behind plan, and green indicates on or ahead of plan. No one has time to read lengthy, verbose financial reports. Finance, in cooperation with business-unit leaders, should compile a brief set of bullets that clearly explain all deviations and what's being done to achieve or improve the plan. If additional information is required you can provide whatever backup is needed. The key is to simply and effectively communicate how the business is performing compared to plan.

You want answers and commitments, not lengthy explanations and excuses. So another effective tool for remaining focused on near-term results is the use of a three-month rolling forecast. The business-unit leaders should develop these forecasts each month in conjunction with finance. Leaders should have a pretty good idea of what needs to happen within ninety days to achieve plan. This tactical focus removes some of the unknowns and guesswork inherent in longer-range forecasts.

Every company must know where profits are being made. Profits should be reported by product, service, line of business, customer, industry, or whatever categories make sense for your company. And it's just as important to know where and why losses are being incurred so you can take action to reverse the situation.

Caution: Do not evaluate results strictly on a consolidated, or rolled-up, basis. When this is done, good results offset poor results, and you can't tell what actions are required to maximize profitability. To this end, finance should publish the key metrics, what I call the significant few: revenue, cash flow, depreciation, accounts receivable, billing quality, inventory turns, market share, expenses, product volumes, product margins, customer churn, head count, win/loss results, refunds/credits, and productivity. Summary reports, as well as reports by business unit and product, should be produced to avoid the roll-up problem. These operating metrics should be examined in addition to standard financial metrics, such as debt-to-equity ratio, current ratio, liability ratios, return on assets, economic value added (EVA), and price-earnings ratios.

I've seen so many companies make the mistake of closely guarding this information. Instead, with the advice of your company's legal counsel, make the information widely available, so that everyone who needs this information knows where the company stands. If you are concerned that this information might fall into the wrong hands, then post results as a percentage of plan.

When employees know the health of the company, it's a lot easier to enlist support the next time changes are required. To accomplish this, managers and the finance team must educate employees on the meaning of each metric and its impact on the company. This approach takes time, but it's well worth it to reduce rumors and keep the focus on the task at hand.

Finance Is Traffic Control

This list illustrates how finance establishes authority procedures across the company.

- **Acquisition authority:** who can commit the company to purchase, and what the levels of authority are
- **Contract authority:** who can sign for the company, and what the levels of authority are
- **Capital allocation:** who decides where and when to make capital investments
- **Financial justification:** how investments are approved (This is a process that must be documented and taught across the company. Just because a project is in the budget doesn't mean the money can be spent. Finance must evaluate and justify expenditures at the time of investment.)
- **Audit process:** when and how to verify that investments yield committed returns
- **Customer credit screening:** what information is required from whom, and when
- **Accounts payable:** determines if the company takes advantage of payment terms and maximizes cash flow
- **Accounts receivable:** how soon is soon enough (Receivables are critical to cash flow. Your business is not a bank. Thresholds for collection must be firm.)
- **Customer billing:** are billings timely and accurate (This is an important point of customer contact, with great influence on customer satisfaction and cash flow. If billing is not accurate, surprises can be costly. Finance can help solve billing problems and prevent disputes on the front end by clearly defining payment terms in advance.)
- **Checks and balances:** ensures that internal financial functions are separated adequately to avoid loss and embezzlement

- **Employee expense reimbursement:** ensures that clear guidelines and policies exist and that an effective audit process is in place

Does Your Finance Team Measure Up?

To help companies evaluate their finance teams, I ask key questions that should each be answered with a resounding *yes!* Here are nine of the most important criteria you can use to evaluate the effectiveness of your finance team.

Does my financial team

1. Proactively provide specific business recommendations to improve company profitability?
2. Accurately capture results, convert data into information, and provide reports that enable effective decision making?
3. Always operate with utmost integrity?
4. Provide real-time data analysis, not thirty to sixty days in arrears?
5. Have a deep understanding of the business that enables them to make qualified, actionable recommendations aimed at achieving the company's profitability objectives?
6. Provide "early warning" information by tracking key internal and external leading indicators to help anticipate changes in the business environment?
7. Ensure adequate and ready access to capital by establishing relationships with multiple sources, maintaining strong banking relationships, and securing capital when times are good?
8. Continually negotiate better terms on all contracts, leases, and vendor agreements?
9. Take a leadership role in the business-planning process?

Very Important Lessons

In my work with companies from many industries, I've learned some lessons that have universal meaning. Here are several of those lessons that will make your financial management team a strong contributor to sustained profitability:

- Know the business.
- Lead, don't follow.
- Know the numbers and provide sound business judgment.
- Act quickly to resolve problems. They will only get worse.
- Speak up loudly when planned results are not being achieved.
- Verify accuracy.
- Enforce policies fairly and universally.
- Teach financial justification processes across the company.
- Ensure adequate access to capital.
- Be prepared for the worst case.
- Be a healthy skeptic.

ACTIONS TO TAKE NOW

Stop and take a moment to write down your responses to the following:

1. Who in your company or organization takes a leadership role in the business-planning process? Who else should be included? How can you get them to participate?
2. Does your financial team track leading internal and external indicators that help management anticipate changes in the business environment? If not, what can you do to improve this situation?
3. Does your financial team provide you with the information you need to make accurate and timely decisions? If not, what steps will you take to get this information?
4. Are you satisfied with the accuracy of your financial forecasts? If not, what actions will you take to improve accuracy?

Financial management guides you toward achieving and accelerating profitability, yet winners also have something else going for them to improve forecast accuracy. We move on to the fifth attribute of highly profitable companies—customer loyalty.

SIX

Customer Loyalty: The Win That Keeps On Giving

Having loyal customers reduces uncertainty and improves the confidence you can have in financial forecasts. It's also far more cost-effective and efficient to keep existing customers than it is to acquire new ones. Loyal customers are a source for testing new products and services, as well as a tremendous source of quality introductions. And loyal customers are resistant to competitive inroads, which leads to increased customer share that keeps you in the winner's circle.

Numerous books, research studies, and examples of companies are available to illustrate excellent customer service. So why does customer loyalty remain such an elusive quality for so many companies? We all know how real and pervasive customer loyalty problems are—just listen to the experiences unhappy customers are so willing to share. Stories abound of gross incompetence, missed appointments, wrong products delivered, incorrect billing, rudeness, ineffective communications, passing the buck, and on and on. How many times do you hear people say, I will never use them again?

It's gotten to the point where poor service is the norm and great customer service is the exception. Although we're all well aware of this reality, are you certain how your company performs?

A lot of lip service is paid to customer loyalty in corporate America. Some corporate gurus call it "customer delight," others preach "the customer is always right" or "the customer comes first." Yet you'd be surprised how often I find the majority of a company's employees don't understand why they're chanting the company customer service mantra, because management has never explained to them exactly what having loyal customers really means to the bottom line. Nor have top executives said what actions and resources are required to achieve the customer service objective.

When I ask leaders to state their company's top objectives, they almost always include something about customer satisfaction. Yet few can sufficiently quantify their objectives in this area. It's not good enough to declare you want to have great customer satisfaction or improve customer satisfaction. With vague objectives like these, you'll never know if you're achieving them.

State customer-satisfaction objectives in terms of numbers of customers who will provide testimonials and referrals, the amount of repeat business, or a specific increase in the percentage of business you conduct with certain customers. For greater precision, establish ever-increasing goals by measuring the percentage change in the number of clients who evaluate your company as meeting or exceeding their expectations.

It's not difficult to strengthen customer loyalty. It only takes perseverance, attention to detail, and a good road map. This chapter is designed to give you the essential elements required to build or strengthen your customer loyalty.

One important section of the studies conducted by The Prosen Center for Business Advancement asks senior executives to evaluate their company's customer service and support. Here are some of the results of one recent survey:

Strengths

- We resolve customer problems quickly: 77 percent.
- We know what we have to do to maintain a loyal customer base: 66 percent.
- We proactively elicit customer feedback: 63 percent.

Weaknesses

- We test our customer service/support often; for example, by having an employee pose as a customer: 5 percent.
- We capture the reasons behind all service calls, establish a feedback loop to sales, marketing, product development, manufacturing, operations, and finance to improve performance: 32 percent.
- We continually explain ongoing value to existing customers: 39 percent.
- We consistently underpromise and overdeliver: 39 percent.

Harris: We consistently meet customer expectations: 57 percent.

As the results show, it wouldn't require much change to beat your competition by making adjustments in these key areas of weakness.

The following section shows you how to lock in customer loyalty. Customer loyalty is the foundation of your business. When the economy is suffering, when you're experiencing product or service problems, or when the competition is tough—and it always is—customer loyalty will help keep you alive. Without it, all you have is transactions. With it, instead of needing to focus solely on how many new customers you need to make plan, you can focus on how you can increase your business with your existing customers. When you have true customer loyalty, your customers will stay with you even when times are tough. They won't easily succumb to competitive pressures, because you've differentiated yourself to the point that they never think of straying.

When the dot-com bust hit, I experienced the power of customer loyalty with one of the companies I ran. For several months the sales force was unable to close enough new customers to meet quota. Thankfully, we had a very loyal customer base that kept buying from us through the tough times. These were the customers who kept the company in business.

If you aren't taking care of your existing customers, you're just spinning your wheels. I've never completely understood why companies allow their customers to become dissatisfied. In almost every case, the problems leading to dissatisfaction could have been avoided. Companies spend tremendous resources on sales and marketing to acquire new customers, yet frequently the same effort is not made to retain them.

If you are taking care of customers and your relationships are solid, you'll find you can grow your business more predictably. When you serve your customers well, you can plan with confidence because you know their needs and how to fill them. In fact, loyal customers expect you to provide them with the products and services they need day-to-day.

Harris: We set goals that please our customers: 63 percent.

It's vital to your company's future for everyone—from top managers to line workers—to understand this imperative and the serious ramifications of customer churn. After all, it doesn't take much to ruin customer relationships—and so many people in a company have the opportunity to do it, not just those with direct customer interaction. Once employees understand why customer loyalty is so important, you can begin to talk about how you get it.

Every point of customer contact is an opportunity to either strengthen or erode loyalty. When companies handle service issues quickly, accurately, and with minimal hand-offs, and then give special attention to follow-up, they build loyalty through positive experiences. That little extra touch of follow-up doesn't have to be expensive to pay off big. For instance, you can send thank you notes or proactively make post-service or post-sales calls to ensure expectations were met. Once again, we all know this, but not enough companies do it.

Do you know the specific reasons behind every customer loss? I ask this question a lot and generally receive anecdotal responses. Few leaders track the root causes of why they lose customers. Remember how I noted in the chapter on operational excellence that this was one of the most common areas in business that can benefit from RCA and ICA. Now you know why. It's impossible to reduce customer loss unless you fully understand why customers leave. As a leader, you should receive a monthly report that details how well your company is performing in this critical area and what actions are required to strengthen customer loyalty.

So, how do you determine if customers are loyal? The answer is locked inside two questions, and you must be able answer a resounding *yes!* to both: Will they continue to buy from you? Will they provide quality introductions and testimonials?

If you can't answer affirmatively to both of these questions at any time with every customer, take immediate action to develop a loyal customer base.

There are also a number of key questions you should regularly ask your existing customers: What can we do to better serve you? What do you want more of? What do we need to do to win more of your business?

Remember, asking these questions is just the beginning. Taking action on the answers is where you begin to build customer loyalty.

Later in this chapter, I'll discuss various methods for collecting customer loyalty information and using it to strengthen loyalty.

Focus on Creating Profitable Customers for Life

To do this, you must first focus your entire organization—not just your customer service unit—on the primary objective of creating profitable customers for life who will provide quality introductions to future customers.

Does the following story sound familiar? You and a colleague are in a meeting with a prospective client when you're asked to provide three references. You respond by saying that you will send three names as soon as you get back to the office. When you leave the meeting, you ask your colleague if you have three customers who will give you strong testimonials without having to call them in advance.

When asked for references, wouldn't it be a lot more effective to immediately hand the prospective client a list of twenty customers he or she can call at any time? The best way to accomplish this is to set a goal of having 100 percent referenceable customers.

To strengthen loyalty and gain quality introductions and testimonials, your company must do the following six things well:

1. Sell reliable products and services
2. Make and meet commitments
3. Underpromise and overdeliver
4. Resolve problems quickly
5. Minimize surprises
6. Follow up

I'm often asked if customer loyalty should be with sales or in a different department. The answer varies by company. In general, sales should be responsible for the overall relationship and be kept informed of any significant events. But day-to-day responsibility should lie with operations or customer service and not with sales. Companies that task their sales organization with responsibilities that take them away from selling reduce their chances for making the top line. I have seen too many companies shift service problems, order tracking, and accounts receivable onto their sales team and then wonder why quota is not being achieved. Your delivery organizations—operations, account management, or customer service—should maintain customer relations and be accountable for customer loyalty. If your products and services are not reliable, improve them.

I am also a firm believer in holding all senior management accountable for improving customer loyalty. It takes the entire company to solidify customer loyalty. The best way to do this is to tie a meaningful portion of executive compensation to meeting specific customer-loyalty objectives. Include many leaders of your company or organization in this linkage: executive management; the heads of sales, operations, and customer service and support; managers within customer service and support arenas; and account management departments.

Communicate Openly and Honestly

Good communication—both internal and external—is essential to achieving customer loyalty. Internally, take all customer feedback seriously and encourage employees at all levels to share customer responses. One of the best ways to accomplish this is to determine the specific type of information you want to capture and which departments are responsible for its collection.

For instance, your sales force knows when a customer is considering another supplier or has an issue with your company's product or service. Customer service knows exactly why customers contact them. And finance knows all about billing and accounts-receivable issues. This information is easily captured and should be shared in monthly, cross-functional meetings. Once shared, you can triangulate on customer issues and take proactive steps to avoid or minimize customer defection.

You interact with your customers on multiple levels and with a number of different people, all of whom talk about your service. That's why you have to gather information from all touch points within your company. In this way, you can get an accurate understanding of how your customers view your product or service. Armed with this information, you can take specific actions to address issues, minimize surprises, and strengthen loyalty.

The information you gather is extremely useful, not only to eliminate future problems, but also to gain insight into new products and services. It's also a great way to gather competitive intelligence and better understand the customer decision-making process. Be sure to establish formal feedback loops to regularly share detailed information with sales, marketing, and product development. Casual conversation based on anecdotal information doesn't lead to meaningful action.

Externally, handle disputes and emergencies with exceptional service, honesty, and constant communication through status reports and follow-up. Though this means you must sometimes communicate bad news, it minimizes surprises, which are a quick way to lose a customer.

Being honest with your customers is essential. Honesty must be a visible facet of your corporate culture. Everyone must understand that when a problem arises, it's best to fully disclose it. Then address how it will be solved and when, giving a realistic time frame. Customers respect honesty and forthrightness because it demonstrates commitment and integrity.

I know firsthand the importance of integrity. One of my clients is a large independent school district, which, like other organizations, has a defined contract-approval process with specific spending limits. While in a meeting, I was presented with a check in payment for my services. However, I declined the check because I was concerned the district might have unknowingly exceeded their approved budget for this project. I asked them to withhold payment until they were certain the amount was within their spending limit. A couple of weeks later I received payment along with sincere appreciation for bringing the issue to their attention and for waiting to receive payment until proper authorization was obtained.

When a problem occurs, you can't overcommunicate. Tell customers what happened, why it happened, how it is being corrected, and, most importantly, how you are going to prevent it from happening again. When problems affect multiple customers simultaneously, communicate a consistent message. Don't allow various internal groups to develop their own messages. Designate someone centrally to construct a consistent message and provide it to your company for dissemination.

It's so tempting to avoid full disclosure when you're dealing with embarrassing mistakes. But customers are smart. They know when a situation is not going well. If you explain the issues, acknowledge mistakes, and state what you are doing to minimize the impact and reduce the chance of the problem recurring, more often than not you'll retain customers.

But here's the catch: don't allow the same problem to keep happening. This erodes confidence and makes you vulnerable to the competition. This is why you should insist on RCA and ICA in your company.

I once had a customer who was so upset with our service because of repeated problems that the only possible way to retain the business was for the CEO to personally call their president every day to review the steps we were taking to fulfill our service guarantee. Thankfully, after several weeks of calls and no more service interruptions, we were able to end the daily calls. Sometimes it takes this level of effort to retain customers. Unfortunately for us, it was an expensive lesson to learn.

Another important time to communicate is when change is coming. Change gives you the opportunity to show customers how important they are to your business, by proactively taking the time to tell them what's going on and how it will affect them. Don't surprise your customers if there is *any* way to avoid it. Whenever possible, advise them in advance. It pays big dividends.

Exceed Expectations

Top customer service departments go beyond delivering what's expected. Not only do they keep their customers top-of-mind, they also think about their customers' customers. Exceptional customer service teams continuously look for new ways to help their existing customers increase their business. And they never stop communicating their value proposition. They understand the adage "out of sight, out of mind."

> *Harris:* We consistently meet the expectations of our customers: 57 percent.

Behind the scenes, the best companies constantly perform miracles for their customers that are never disclosed. If you want to increase your value and distance yourself from the competition, inform customers of what your company does to provide them with excellent service. You can accomplish this in several ways. You can create a newsletter or send a monthly or quarterly personalized report. For larger customers, you might schedule formal reviews to discuss all aspects of your relationship, including the things you do for them behind the scenes. Few companies do this, because it takes extra effort. However, if customer retention and loyalty are important to you, you will make this a priority.

It's especially important to go above and beyond with your top customers. Concentrate sufficient resources to provide your very best service to them. Highly profitable companies understand that top customers are the ones they can't afford to lose.

Your best customers value what you provide, rarely question pricing, and at the end of the day, their business is always profitable.

A good example of how a top Dallas law firm differentiates themselves on service is by consistently exceeding client expectations. Whenever they commit to a due date, extra time is built in to ensure they always deliver at least one day ahead of schedule. It sure would be nice if all companies operated that way.

If customers aren't profitable for you, take one of three actions:

1. Provide a different level of service that doesn't require as many resources.
2. Renegotiate terms.
3. Phase out those customers.

Don't retain customers who don't make you money. Eventually they'll rob time and resources from your good customers. Ask your finance team to determine which customers are profitable and which ones require a different relationship or need to be phased out.

Keeping profitable customers for life doesn't imply acting as the bank. Once you have fulfilled your obligations you should be paid according to the terms of the agreement. Any delays should be professionally and aggressively pursued. Don't confuse the need to maintain good relations with the need to achieve your company's financial objectives. Staying current on accounts receivable and not extending terms beyond policy avoids future problems that are inevitably harder to solve.

Consistently Measure Customer Loyalty, and Then Act On It

Highly profitable companies invest significant resources in measuring customer loyalty. They establish a stable customer-survey process to develop reliable trends, and they purposefully use the information to strengthen customer loyalty.

Fewer than 65 percent of companies even measure customer satisfaction, let alone loyalty. Just think how you can use this to your advantage. If you would like a free customer loyalty survey that contains the two most important questions to determine a customer's loyalty, you can obtain one online from my Web site at www.bobprosen.com/loyaltysurvey.

Collecting customer loyalty information can be difficult, but it's a critical step. One of the most common methods is to use a survey. Unfortunately, most people don't like filling out surveys, especially if there are more than a dozen questions. You have to keep surveys short and to the point. It's also important to know who you want to complete the survey and to include multiple people within the same company in order to get a complete picture. You also might want to consider using an outside firm to conduct the survey. Top survey firms conduct extensive phone interviews with your most important customers. They are expert at determining how well your company performs at all levels, as well as pinpointing customer needs and how to best meet customer expectations and strengthen your relationship. Sometimes people won't be as candid with you as they would be with a third party.

Surveys can be mailed or done over the telephone. For your most important clients, you might want to meet with them in person to discuss your company's performance. Someone in your company who doesn't have direct day-to-day contact with customers should do this.

I suggest conducting a formal survey once a year. You also might want to conduct minisurveys around certain events, such as the completion of a project. Once you collect the data, it's easy to compile it using a bar or line graph. The goal is to show improvement over time, and using graphs is an effective way to evaluate progress. If you are not satisfied with the results, find out why by using RCA and ICA to eliminate the problems once and for all.

What's most important is that you use the information collected to enact improvements and provide feedback to your customers and employees. Explain the importance of this process to customers so they understand that their participation ensures the continuous improvement of products and services. When customers and employees believe the information is being used for their benefit, they will continue to support the process. If not, the process will fail.

Do Your Customer Service and Support Measure Up?

To help companies evaluate their own customer service and support, I teach executives how to ask key questions, which should each be answered with a resounding *yes!* Here are seven of the most important criteria you can use to evaluate your customer service and support.

Do we

1. Consistently underpromise and overdeliver?
2. Resolve customer problems quickly?
3. Take all customer feedback seriously?
4. Have a process in place to reduce problem recurrence?
5. Consistently measure customer loyalty and improve results?
6. Know what each person at the company must do to maintain a loyal customer base?
7. Continually explain ongoing value to existing customers?

Very Important Lessons

My work with numerous companies across industries has taught me some customer service lessons that have universal meaning. Taking these steps will make your customer service team a strong contributor to sustained profitability:

- Test your customer service and support process often.
- Link key customers with senior executives to deepen relationships.
- Be proud of your service and charge accordingly.
- Communicate effectively and fulfill commitments as promised.
- Keep in touch.
- Strive to have 100 percent of your customers referenceable.
- Overcommunicate in times of trouble.
- Don't become a bank for your customers. Collect outstanding receivables aggressively.

ACTIONS TO TAKE NOW

There are several actions to take to strengthen your company's customer loyalty. Ask yourself these questions:

1. How loyal are your customers? If you don't know, what steps will you take to find out?
2. Does everyone who needs to maintain customer loyalty know how to do it? If not, what are you going to do about it and when?
3. How many existing customers will give you positive references and testimonials?
4. How many new customers did you gain over the past twelve months, and from what specific sources?
5. How many customers stopped doing business with your company over the past twelve months, and for what reasons?

You now have a basic understanding of The Five Attributes of Highly Profitable Companies:

1. Superior leadership
2. Sales effectiveness
3. Operational excellence
4. Financial management
5. Customer loyalty

It's time to put them to work. Part III will take you step-by-step from planning into action, teaching you how to execute your plan and truly accelerate profitability and achieve extraordinary results.

PART THREE

Execute for Results

CHAPTER 7

Bridging the Gap

At the beginning of the day, it's all about possibilities.
At the end of the day, it's all about results.

The true measure of a business's success is its ability to understand this mantra, and as a consequence, continuously meet or exceed its profitability objectives. The biggest challenges in business are neither planning nor strategy but the ability to execute and stay focused on achieving your plan.

In this section I'll talk about execution, taking you from planning through execution to your acceleration of profitability.

I define execution as the way you achieve your objectives. It's about getting things done and making results happen.

Companies allocate sizable resources to planning. The resulting documents are testimony to business acumen and cogent

Harvard Business Review on Entrepreneurship (Boston, MA: Harvard Business School Press, 1999) provided some ideas for a small section of this chapter.

thinking. They are most often the work products of dedicated, talented management and creative consultants. But—and this is a big but—too often in corporate America, the objectives in these plans are not achieved.

Why not? Because progress is not consistently tracked or reported, shortfalls are not taken seriously, excuses and rationalization are the norm, and commitments are either not made or no one follows through with them. In short, there is a lack of accountability.

When you drill deeper, what's really happening is that the company is stuck in one or more of the five crippling habits I addressed in chapter 2. All too often, companies return to the drawing board instead of concentrating on taking action to meet their objectives. Unless you avoid or immediately stop this wasteful cycle, you will compromise your company's profitability.

Sometimes the problem is that leaders plan on achieving perfection, which is impossible. The unforeseen happens. Markets change. So you must plan for change and remain flexible. If you don't plan for change, you're liable to find your business in a declining profit cycle. When results are not continuously compared to plan, you can end up having to make big cost-cutting adjustments late in the game.

Unfortunately, the easiest number to fix is the one associated with people. Last-minute layoffs may balance the budget, but they also set companies up for disaster. The impact of layoffs on morale and stockholder confidence is profound. Ultimately it drives loss of faith in leadership and complacency and opens the door for talented people to look for new opportunities.

Most leaders know what they want. The challenge is getting the company to execute with speed and efficiency to consistently deliver the desired results.

The key is to bridge the gap between planning and results by executing effectively. We achieve objectives in that gap between vision and reality, between mapping the adventure and arriving at the destination. But before we develop the link between the plan and the results, it's important to understand an effective plan's essential elements.

First Choose Your Direction

Your strategy must provide clear direction in concise language that's easily understood by employees, shareholders, and customers alike. In your strategy, state where the company is headed instead of where it is. And don't be so broad that the company has wide latitude. Instead, provide a structure for decision making and establishing policy. Your strategy sets boundaries that guide you in making the decisions required to meet your company's financial goals. To be successful, your strategy has to consistently meet your customers' needs better than the competition and lead your business to marketplace success.

Here are some examples of clear strategy and mission statements from well-known companies:

> **3M:** To solve unsolved problems innovatively
>
> **Wal-Mart:** To give ordinary folk the opportunity to buy the same things as rich people
>
> **Nike:** To bring inspiration and innovation to every athlete in the world
>
> **Disney:** To make people happy

It's vital for a company's top leaders to develop the strategy. Don't delegate this task. Even though ultimately you will set the direction, gather input from key constituencies, including customers, shareholders, management, and employees. If it is to be a clear directive, however, it can't be the aggregation of many people's opinions. Remember, you can't be everything to everyone.

If you think you have a good strategy in place, test it. Ask yourself many tough questions. Begin by asking if you can achieve your profitability objectives. In other words, did you pick the right goals on which to concentrate your resources? To determine this, you have to assess your competitive advantage. Are you truly better than your competition? Have you sufficiently differentiated your product or service to charge a premium? How do you know?

This inquiry leads you directly to your customer base. Do you understand your existing customer base and your market? Why do customers buy your products or services rather than your competitors'? Once you know for certain, focus your resources on producing what will allow you to grow. Remember, your customers can't always tell you exactly what they need. You also have to be creative.

When I was the chief operating officer of a leading Web-hosting company, I worked for an exceptionally creative CEO who had a knack for knowing what customers needed before they knew themselves. He listened to customers, anticipated their needs, and used his deep understanding of technology to develop solutions that allowed the company to always stay several steps ahead of the competition.

As you articulate your strategic goals, you need to know if your market is growing or shrinking. Remember that it's easier to gain market share in a growing market. If the market is static or shrinking, then you have to steal market share from competitors who have the advantage of established customer relationships. And that's much harder.

When you plan, begin with your existing strategy. If this strategy doesn't produce sufficient profits, then you must either reduce your cost structure or develop a more profitable strategy. Either way, take specific actions. Don't sit around and wait for something good to happen. The "we could get lucky" approach will only get you into deeper trouble. Deconstruct what's wrong and fix it or get out.

Is Your Competitive Advantage Sustainable?

All products and services can be imitated. Just because you have a great idea doesn't mean it's sustainable. Whenever there is profit or a positive NPV in a market, any market, competition will enter. This is a universal truth, so get ready for it. Someone is going to come in and try to take some of what you've got. So, if your products and services are easy to duplicate, get busy developing distinctive processes that enable you to differentiate in a unique way. If your company is strong at developing relationships with customers and channel partners, that's hard to duplicate. If you can execute better and bring new products and services to market more quickly and less expensively, or your quality is substantially better than your competitors', that's hard to copy. If you have tools and processes that allow you to solve problems quicker and less expensively, that's a powerful advantage. Another great way to build barriers to entry is through patents. Determine what will give you a sustainable advantage, and then do it. This is often referred to as an unfair competitive advantage.

You can gain another key advantage by learning everything you can about your competition. Know their leadership. Who are they? Where did they come from? How do they think? Study them. What have they done in the past and how well? Are they fully funded? What's their strategy? How do they differentiate themselves? What do they depend on to make their strategy sustainable? How do they respond to competition? It's a competitive war, and you need to win. Know your competition so you can beat them.

Competitive intelligence is a process, not a one-time event. Do not allow your competition to surprise you. Remember, once you implement your strategy, it's hard to change. You don't want to set it in motion and then learn that your competition has a better strategy. Here are a few examples: VHS versus Betamax;

low-cost airlines, such as Southwest Airlines and JetBlue, versus full-service carriers; Japanese automakers versus the Big Three; digital media versus film, and online music stores versus bricks-and-mortar stores.

Are Your Growth Objectives Attainable?

All strategies are based on assumptions, such as how fast the market or the competition is growing. To know whether your growth objectives are realistic, first understand that it's a heck of a lot easier to grow when your customers are loyal. With customer loyalty you automatically improve your chances of achieving your growth goals because there is less churn, and you can depend on your customers to stick with you.

Next understand what drives profit in your business. For example, if your profit growth depends on scale—producing more and selling more—then you'd better be in a market that's growing. If you can't grow, you won't reach the economies of scale required to meet your profitability objectives. So, you have to understand the mechanics of your business.

You also need to know if you have enough resources to accomplish your goals. Do you have the right people with the right talent? Do you have enough of the right capital and technology to execute? The last thing you want to do is create a plan and jump into it only to discover you don't have adequate resources to execute. The advice I give leaders is to secure more funding than they need because it always costs more to achieve your goals than you originally thought.

If your plan is to be self-funded, meaning you don't want to borrow or obtain outside investments, then you must limit your growth to match your internal funding. This automatically establishes thresholds that mean you can't grow as fast as you could with external capital.

Finally, to determine whether your growth goals are realistic, you must be able to generate increasing positive net cash flow. I'm not talking about EBITDA (earnings before interest, taxes, depreciation, and amortization). Many companies make the mistake of only setting targets for revenue growth and market share as indicators of success. That strategy is shortsighted and will eventually compromise your business. You should only grow as fast as you can grow profitably. Never confuse revenue and growth with profit and cash flow.

Have I Hired the Right People?

This is critically important. It's essential to have the right people in the right positions, people who are smarter than you in their respective areas of responsibility. Unless you are prepared to invest in underperformers, you are better off finding them a different position either in or out of the company. To determine the feasibility of your plan and reach your ultimate strategic goal, it's vitally important to have the right people. Leaders must do whatever it takes to make the perfect match. This is the foundation for success.

I am often asked what was the one thing I have done that had the biggest impact on results. My reply is always the same. I hire people smarter than I am and put them in the right positions. Then I let them perform.

Is your culture right for achieving your plan? Can your team work together and stay focused on the best way for the company to achieve its objectives? For the culture to be right, you must make it accountability based, and you need to minimize politics and self-preservation tactics. As a result, you greatly increase the odds for achieving your goals. Culture is simply the way things get done in an organization, the spoken and unspoken rules of behavior. Typically, there is no policy and procedures manual that accurately describes culture, because culture permeates and transcends written rules. It's how people work together, how well they handle change, and how they manage in a crisis.

You must understand that culture is not something that just happens. A company's leaders always establish its culture, either knowingly or unknowingly. You must nurture and mold a culture into what you want it to be. It's difficult to achieve a results-driven culture, and it's a never-ending process to maintain. But the return on investment is worth the trouble.

In an organization where knowledge is power, where internal competition is rewarded, where empire building is condoned, where communication is lacking and self-interest is prominent, it's almost impossible to reach your objectives. This shark mentality breeds victims in an environment where personal agendas are more important than the company's agenda. I have witnessed this type of behavior in many companies, and it all begins and ends with the leader.

I recall sitting in the president's office of a major telecommunications company one evening when he turned to me and said, "If I stand in front of the main entrance at five minutes to five, I'll be trampled by employees leaving the office. Why am I working so hard when everyone else is leaving early?" My reply was simple: "People are following the culture that you established. If you don't like it, change it." Unfortunately, he never addressed the issue, which, when combined with other problems, resulted in several significant workforce reductions.

Conversely, companies that reward accountability and results, and cultivate open, honest communication, can unite to discuss problems, seek the best solutions, assist team members who are struggling, and work together to consistently achieve objectives. This type of culture emphasizes that winning means the entire company is successful. Such companies understand that everyone is dependent on one another and that the whole business is seamlessly intertwined.

Evaluate your company by these standards so that you can quickly determine where you stand.

Do you hear a lot of "we" or more "I" in conversations? Is the underlying motivation, "What's in it for me?" or "What's in it for us?" A healthy culture is collaborative and supportive. It's about being accountable to one another and requesting and giving help. It's not about demonstrating that you're the brightest person in the room.

Debate Your Assumptions

List every assumption included in your plan—how fast you think the market will grow, how much market share you think you can get, time to market, your sources of intellectual capital, the capability and capacity of internal processes, competitive responses, future economic conditions, and the availability of financial capital. These are vital factors. After all, a plan is called a plan because it's based on assumptions and forecasts. Otherwise it would be called an *actual.*

Kick your assumptions around a lot with your P&L owners to make certain that your assumptions are valid. Make sure you've based them on data that your whole team can buy into. If you can't debate and thoroughly agree on the assumptions, then you won't get buy-in to your plan.

I work with many companies that don't do this. Instead, assumptions are determined at the top. This gives everyone down the line an excuse to fail because there's no ownership. Here is the key: once the debate is done, the leader makes the final call and everyone lines up to meet the plan.

Analyze Risk

Analyzing risk is another essential factor for creating a good plan. Risk is inherent in every business and can't be eliminated totally.

Therefore I always advise business leaders to take calculated risks, not unbridled chances. It makes a lot more sense to minimize risk whenever possible. Too many things come up that are beyond your control, so control the ones you can.

You have to identify the possible roadblocks ahead and, more importantly, what you will do if they materialize. For instance, let's say you plan to introduce a new product. What would the company do if your competition introduced essentially the same product six months sooner? Have you differentiated yourself enough? Are your customers loyal enough to wait for your product? You must anticipate these circumstances so that if they happen, you're not saying to yourself, *I wish we had thought about that.*

Another example is, if you assume interest rates of 6 percent, what will you do if they jump to 12 percent? Here you may be looking at hedge fund strategies or other ways of mitigating risk. I also suggest every company answer the question, "Where are we vulnerable and how do we prevent the competition from taking advantage?" Risk analysis is important, but you don't have to get bogged down in worrying about all of the possibilities. Just grab the biggest ones and figure out how you would respond to them. One way to assess risk is to assume that the worst has already occurred. Then look back and ask yourself what you could have done to prevent the occurrence or minimize the impact. Depending on the probability of a significant event actually occurring, you might want to implement preventive measures in advance. In my workshops I help business leaders and managers develop an early-warning system to minimize financial surprises, quantify their top objectives and develop action plans to achieve them, connect the entire organization to the top objectives, solve problems, and respond to change.

At this point you should have your strategy and business plan in place, with primary objectives and the right leadership on board. Now it's time to develop your operating plan, how you will achieve your objectives.

Convert Plans into Actions

Operating plans are tactical in nature. They spell out the steps every organization must take to achieve the business plan. This is where you begin to bridge the gap between planning and results. An operating plan must be measurable and highlight key milestones to achieve throughout the year. Your operating plan is a road map that tells you how you execute your business plan. It's an instrument that shows if you are staying on course.

Leaders responsible for delivering results must develop operating plans. They can't and won't buy into these plans if others developed them. Leaders have to lay out the specific programs, timelines, measurements, and resources required to achieve their objectives, which, in turn, are aligned with the company's overall objectives.

Once the operating plan is developed, it needs a budget. Combining the budget with an actionable operating plan is an iterative process that enables you to prioritize projects, say no to less important initiatives, link resources, and quantify specific deliverables by individual employees. This is powerful stuff. It's the direct connection between objectives and results, with touch points throughout your business.

When the business plan, the operating plan, and the budget come together, you know precisely what you want to accomplish, how you're going to do it, who is responsible, what it's going to cost, and how you're going to meet your financial and operating objectives. When combined with an effective measurement and reward system, this becomes the most powerful way to establish accountability across your entire company and achieve results.

Once you bring your plan to this point, it can be translated quickly down the line into specific objectives for every individual.

Ultimately you should have a direct line of sight from individual objectives through the operational plan to the business plan and the company's financial performance. Every person in your company should know exactly how his or her individual objectives tie directly to the success of the business. The concept that everyone is part of a larger process becomes part of your holistic culture.

With this mind-set, employees can know how they impact sales, costs, quality, production, customer loyalty, and, ultimately, profitability. Once you have accomplished this, you will be in a position to ask employees the two questions addressed in the chapter on superior leadership: What are the company's top business goals? What are you doing today to accomplish them?

Have all the pieces in place on January 1 or by the beginning of your company's fiscal year. Too many companies lock their plans down sometime during the first quarter. Never allow this to happen to you. Be ready on January 1 or the first day of your fiscal year. The best-led companies start the planning process in the third quarter to build the framework for the next year. When they come out of the gate, they have 365 days to achieve their plan.

But you're not finished planning on December 31, because on January 31 it's time to reevaluate. Continuous reevaluation is part of the process. Don't make it difficult. Planning reviews should be part of your company's culture and should mainly focus on deviations from the plan. Make certain you hold your finance team responsible for creating the planning schedule and ensuring that deadlines are met.

If you're ahead of plan, analyze why. Revisit your planning assumptions. Did the landscape change? What assumptions changed, and will the trend continue? It's important to know the answers to these questions because too much growth can overstretch your company and negatively impact other parts of the business.

View negative deviations the same way. First, what is the deviation? Second, are the assumptions still valid? Third, what specific actions will be taken immediately so the company can return to plan and maintain profitability?

With any negative deviation, regardless of size, it's important to get back on track as quickly as possible. Don't wait to take corrective action, or you may never recover lost ground. Planning reviews can be as frequent as once a month. They won't become tedious as long as they focus on deviation and the specific action that will be taken to remain on or ahead of plan. This is not the type of meeting in which the person with the best story or the one who best explains the deviation wins.

Focus exclusively on the source of all deviations and what you will do to get back on plan. There is no place here for rationalization or victim mentality. When you surround yourself with experts, you will get answers and actions, not excuses. Your culture should create a supportive environment to help everyone stay on track by offering resources across the organization. This is only possible if company leaders understand that success is declared when the entire company reaches its goals.

In the end, it's all about making choices and executing to plan. It's important to make the right choices when you launch a strategy. Even if you execute well, if you've chosen the wrong things to do, ultimately you can't be profitable. With every business, there's always more to accomplish than there are resources and time. So you have to stay focused on the significant few—the most important goals.

ACTIONS TO TAKE NOW

Here are some important actions to take now that will help you achieve your objectives. Please write down your responses.

1. Is your company or organization on plan? If not, what are you doing about it?
2. Are your directions clear, and how do you know all your employees are focused on achieving the company's top objectives?
3. How can you increase accountability and create a results-focused culture?
4. How accurate are your planning assumptions, and what actions will you take to increase their accuracy?
5. In what areas do you need better people? What will you do about these needs, and when will you do it?

This brings us to the next vital step in executing for results: clarifying objectives and establishing priorities. It's time to focus!

EIGHT

Be Your Competitors' Worst Fear

Your competitors' biggest fear isn't so much your bright ideas but your ability to turn those ideas into bottom-line results. That requires an accountability-based culture relentlessly focused on achieving clear goals.

In an accountability-based culture supercharged for action, you shouldn't have to tell anyone *how* to do his or her job, but just *what* needs to be done. If you've hired smart, made certain your team understands the objectives, put the right people in the right jobs so they can fully use their skills, and empowered them to do what they do best, then you should rarely have to get involved in *how* things actually get done.

Of course, it's your job to always be available as a sounding board or to offer suggestions when roadblocks are inevitably encountered. You should also ask probing questions, attend results-review meetings, and teach team members problem-solving and critical-thinking skills. Accountable organizations that consistently achieve their goals and objectives—sans false starts, rework, and political infighting—will outexecute their competition time after time. Once achieved, dependable execution becomes a powerful differentiator that's extremely hard to replicate.

The Power of Commitment

Part of what drives an accountability-based culture is unyielding commitment and belief in the company's primary objectives. Everyone must believe in the mission and agree that the chosen path is right.

To test this commitment within your company, get into the habit of walking around and talking to people. Get off your beaten path and seek out people you don't regularly encounter. Then simply ask them what they're working on and why they're working on it. Walking around to improve communications is discussed further in the following chapter. The relevance of walking around to this chapter is that you can use this technique to better instill an accountability-based culture. To help accomplish this, determine the following: Can employees tell you how their work directly contributes to achieving their organization's top objectives? Do they understand why they're doing what they're doing? Can they explain the company's objectives in their own language, or do they simply regurgitate a mantra?

If they can't do these things and do them well, pay attention. Look deeper. This is exactly where superior leadership makes a difference. These seemingly small adjustments add up, and if they are not addressed, they grow into big problems that are much harder to solve. Most often this is caused by a breakdown in communication or commitment.

Generally, middle management is the key breakdown to successful execution of objectives. Middle managers bridge the gap between the plan and what employees should be working on every day.

The Power of Ownership

I believe in creating an accountability-based culture that assigns personal ownership in order to make things happen. If you break down your operating plans into monthly, weekly, and even daily objectives—each with measurable tasks—and those daily objectives and tasks are assigned and tracked to a single owner, you'll make progress toward achieving your ultimate goals.

> *Harris:* I take individual initiative and responsibility for results: 43 percent.

Assign ownership to everyone from senior-level managers to line workers. Why? Because in this kind of culture it's extremely difficult for blame and victim mentality to take root and grow. Instead, individual owners are forced to be accountable for achieving their goals. If they don't, there's no one else to blame. And if tasks are measured regularly, and the results are accessible for all to see, it's easy to determine when objectives have been met. Public accountability is a powerful motivator.

To ensure accountability, it's critical for actions to have assigned due dates. Then everyone knows not only who owns the action item, but also when commitments must be met. These milestones should be captured in progress reports and measurement systems that are open for review.

The next step toward ensuring accountability is to hold regular progress meetings to report on milestones. This is where accountability truly starts to take shape. These meetings shouldn't drag on indefinitely. Keep them concise, swift, and simple. Have each leader check his or her list of milestones and report on whether or not they have been achieved. If so, move on. If not, focus the discussion specifically on what needs to happen to reach the objectives and agree on new due dates.

Don't allow the conversation to shift into deep problem-solving mode. Accept offers to help and make quick recommendations. Then, if need be, schedule a separate meeting to handle the issue in detail. If dates keep slipping, request a meeting with the person responsible, and get to the root cause. Remember these steps:

- Listen carefully
- Ask what's required to achieve the objective
- Don't accept excuses
- Remove roadblocks
- Gain commitment

When milestones are in jeopardy, a sophisticated team member will know to ask for help because he or she understands that achieving the goal is most important. Depending upon the organization's level of sophistication, other team members should offer support to help their colleague accomplish the objectives.

In a team that really works there's no room for victim mentality and "if only" conversations. If you hear that type of conversation, you're in danger of missing objectives. Instead you should be hearing, "This milestone is in jeopardy, so here are the steps we need to take to get there."

In a culture geared for action, people will offer resources without being asked. Focus on solutions, not excuses. Never underestimate the power of the "all for one, one for all" mentality, especially when teamwork is rewarded.

If individuals feel responsible and personally accountable for delivering results regardless of circumstances—even if they have to enlist help from others—then real results and profits are ahead.

DAILY CHECKLIST

from *Kiss Theory Good Bye*

End indecision, increase your productivity, kiss theory good bye and get the results you need.

TAKE THESE SEVEN STEPS EVERY DAY:

1. Give clear directives. Be short, be definitive, and get to the point.
2. Require accountability. Focus on results, not activity.
3. Never rationalize poor performance.
4. Avoid overplanning. When a plan is in place, execute.
5. Embrace change. Search out opportunities to improve your organization and your results.
6. Help every member on the team win.
7. At the end of every day, ask yourself, "Did my actions today help move the organization closer to meeting its objectives?"

The Prosen Center for Business Advancement
www.bobprosen.com (972) 899-2180

THE LEADER'S ROLE

MAKE EVERYONE WHO REPORTS TO YOU WIN!

from *Kiss Theory Good Bye*

FOUR STEPS TO ACHIEVE WINNING RESULTS:

1. Clearly define everyone's objectives, establish quantifiable metrics, and measure performance.

2. Have each person identify the top three barriers to achieving his or her objectives.

3. Agree on specific actions, responsibilities, and time frames to remove or minimize the barriers.

4. Hold everyone accountable for results and disproportionately reward those who achieve their objectives.

Remember, you win when everyone on the team wins!

The Prosen Center for Business Advancement
www.bobprosen.com (972) 899-2180

The Role of Metrics in Accountability

The importance of metrics in accountability is profound. Start by establishing a simple way to measure progress and success. It's best to determine the significant few measurements rather than the important many, and make sure those measurements are accurately taken. Any more than five or six key metrics per department is too many. Don't get caught up in the process. Metrics are only a means to the end. Metrics help to remove the ambiguity, and when shared regularly and posted for the entire company to view, they allow a healthy, competitive spirit to grow.

Harris:

- Measures are visible and accessible to everyone: 35 percent.
- Measures are tracked accurately and openly: 34 percent.

Let's face it, no one likes to lag behind. A high-performance team wants to broadcast its numbers so everyone in the company perceives it as successful. Therefore, it's critical to measure the right variables. With every measurement, ask the question, So what? If the answer doesn't directly tie to achieving one of the company's top objectives, select another metric.

How Meetings Support Accountability

For meetings to be truly effective, the focus must be on results rather than people. Then it's easy for everyone to be hard on performance and easy on the performers. Effective companies don't get personal when concentrating on results attainment. They focus on removing roadblocks that stand in the way of accomplishing the goal, as opposed to the individual's inability to achieve that goal.

Try this simple method to increase accountability and diminish any blame mentality in your culture: Reduce the number of people in every meeting by half. The only people who should attend are those directly involved in achieving the goal that is the subject of the meeting. Make sure the key players are there. Create a results-oriented agenda in advance. Capture action items in the meeting and assign ownership for each one. Then assign deadlines and a time to reconvene to check progress. Meeting adjourned.

Here's an example of a results-oriented agenda:

Customer Retention Team Update
January 21, 20XX
Conference Room 3B
1:30pm–3:00pm

1. 1:30–1:45 Review action items from the December 17 meeting: Jim
2. 1:45–2:00 Present data showing YTD customer losses by category: Mary
3. 2:00–2:20 Discuss root cause analysis results for top customer-loss category: Mary and Peter
4. 2:20–2:45 Agree on appropriate irreversible corrective action to test: Peter and team
5. 2:45–2:50 Recap today's action items: Jim
6. 2:50–3:00 Open discussion and set next meeting date: Team

How many times have you sat in a meeting and worked on your calendar, read your mail, or messaged people on your PDA? The waste is staggering. I know a company that required everyone attending meetings to log in to the computer in order to calculate the fully loaded cost of everyone in the meeting. Throughout the meeting the total cost was posted on the screen so everyone could see how well they were using the company's assets. Treat every meeting just like any other investment, and ask yourself, what is the return?

Leaders of the twelfth largest school district in America, Dallas Independent School District (DISD), take accountability, productivity, and results seriously. After being introduced to my productivity-enhancement tools they immediately adopted them throughout the district. Within weeks the level of accountability dramatically improved. These seemingly small changes have increased meeting effectiveness, improved morale, and brought the focus to achieving results instead of activity.

The Biggest Obstacle: Politics

Politics do have a couple of positive influences. They create the need to bring people together and generate negotiations. There is the potential to build teamwork, trust, and loyalty. ("I'll do that for you if you do this for me.") Politics can teach compromise, because it's impossible for every individual agenda to be fulfilled. It's paramount, however, for everyone to understand that the company's agenda is the first one to be fulfilled.

To put a stop to damaging political behavior, acknowledge it openly, declare that it's unacceptable, make it clear that it's fine to disagree, and require that disagreements be voiced and debated in the open. Only then can you expose and evaluate alternatives and get 100 percent support. After that, debate and discussion are over. There's nothing left to talk about around the watercooler.

When to Say No

Another key aspect of accountability-based leadership is knowing when to say no. Management must lead by example and show that it's not a sign of weakness to say you can't do everything. Then when employees come to management with too much on their plate, it's management's job to help them prioritize. This process is a lot easier when company and individual objectives are clearly understood. Issues of lesser importance become obvious and are the first to be nixed.

Organizational Boundaries

It's also important for leadership to address organizational boundaries. Many organizations blame lack of progress on internal boundaries because leaders too often spend too much time, energy, and company resources on establishing turf. These individual kingdoms breed unhealthy competition that stifles progress toward company results. Your company should be without boundaries. People should be able to cross between functions and departments, soliciting and offering resources as well as information. I'm not suggesting ignoring proper protocol. But protocol should not be a roadblock to progress.

Several years ago I was brought into a company that was losing a lot of money. After a short time, I determined that millions of dollars were being lost because of inadequate internal controls. I immediately asked my team if they knew about the problem, and if so, why it hadn't been addressed. The answer stunned me. They said the executive in charge of that department would not work with them unless someone of equal status in the company brought the issue forward. Sounds absurd, but it happened. I met with that executive right away and reached agreement to change the informal policy.

Improving cross-organizational effectiveness was also one of the top challenges for DISD. When I began working with DISD they had already made substantial progress in setting clear objectives, defining measurements, tracking performance, and implementing a comprehensive performance appraisal system. The next step was to integrate these systems and processes together to improve execution and results. To accomplish this we developed a customized superior leadership and operational excellence training program for the entire leadership team that leveraged the district's existing tools and processes. Throughout the training we demonstrated how to apply specific tools to solve current challenges and move the organization forward. We also caused divisions to work together cross-functionally to address some of the district's most important objectives. After only a few months, divisions began collaborating and communicating at a level that, up until then, had been impossible to accomplish.

When Roadblocks Are Gone but Problems Persist

If you've removed or substantially reduced the roadblocks and your company or organization is still not progressing toward profitability, chances are you have people in the wrong positions. Clearly, people must be given more than one chance to achieve. Then, if they fail repeatedly, it's the leader's job to recognize that these people are in a position to fail and make a change. In retrospect, leaders often say they waited too long to act.

I was once asked by a company to work one-on-one with the vice president of sales, who wasn't making quota. My first order of business was to ask him what was standing in the way of making his numbers. He identified three issues that we resolved in less than thirty days. Without any other roadblocks, he agreed that at the end of sixty days, if he wasn't making quota, it was on him, not the company. As it turned out, before the sixty-day mark, he saw that he was in the wrong position and left on his own to pursue other interests.

Sometimes the roadblock is an internal process issue, price, or product quality. Sometimes it's lack of training. The important point for leaders to understand is that it is their responsibility to quickly identify and remove, within reason, the roadblocks. All that remains should be the person's ability to deliver. This issue is greatly reduced when you hire smart.

If leadership allows this type of situation to linger, it will negatively impact many other areas and infect other employees.

Suboptimal performance is contagious. You have to remove it, not just move it around. If your company's deadweight is being passed from one manager to another, show leadership and take immediate action. Remember, you're being watched and judged on your ability to make the right decisions.

> *Harris:* People are expected to perform at a high level and low performance is unacceptable: 51 percent.

In today's litigious society, many companies believe that ineffective employees hold them hostage. True, there is protocol to follow to protect yourself against a lawsuit. But if you approach the situation by the book, take the emotion and personality out of it, and deal with the issues, you can remove problem people. If you regularly evaluate performance, you're more than halfway there. If you have action plans in place and get employees to buy into their own accountability, it's much easier to document an individual's lack of performance. Then when it's time to show them the door, it's not a surprise to anyone because you've been documenting the lack of progress all along. The key is to be consistent and evenhanded.

> When it comes to managing performance, most leaders say, "I should have taken action sooner."

Leaders who consistently produce extraordinary results regardless of circumstances have something in common—the ability to hold themselves and their entire organization accountable to achieve the stated goals and objectives. Unfailing execution is an intimidating competitive weapon that unnerves the competition and is revered by clients.

ACTIONS TO TAKE NOW

Here's how to keep yourself and your organization focused on execution.

1. List three ways to improve meeting effectiveness. When will you implement these improvements?
2. What will you do to reduce politics within the organization?
3. Do you have employees who need to produce better results or move on? What actions will you take to make certain results improve?
4. How many metrics do you track? If you have too many, which ones will you eliminate to stay focused on the significant few?

Results and accountability are part of your vocabulary, you have a plan in place that translates the company's top objectives into action, and responsibility has been assigned and accepted. Now it's time to move from the basics to the advanced coursework, the role communication plays in accelerating profitability.

NINE

The Critical Path to Getting Things Done

Just when you think you've communicated enough, go back and communicate some more.

All leaders and all companies talk about the importance of communication. So why do so many companies struggle to do it well? If you have any doubt, just ask your employees. Effective communication is common sense but not common practice. The explanation for this is twofold. Either leaders don't actually know how to effectively communicate, or they don't really believe in its power and therefore don't do it. This chapter is dedicated to those leaders who want to communicate for results.

After twenty-five years of working with some of the world's top corporations, I can tell you this: I've never heard employees complain about getting too much good information from management. Employees have an insatiable desire for information, which is why I tell leaders that they need to communicate, communicate, and then communicate some more.

When and how you disclose information to employees is at the root of making progress toward your top objectives, because communication is the glue that holds the company together. The better you communicate, the more trust you will create, which leads to increased commitment, action, and ultimately results. If any of those components are missing, the connection breaks down and either execution will slow to a halt or, even worse, you won't achieve your objectives.

Inside a company, communication is the critical path to getting things done. Nothing is more powerful. Your company is a network of interdependent commitments and actions all linked by communication. Communication facilitates both commitment and accountability.

> When communication breaks down, commitment and accountability weaken, problems go unaddressed, and ultimately results fall short of the desired outcome.

The most important aspect of good communication is that it begins at the top. Senior management sets the communication style that's acceptable for the company. It's vital that communication is precise and free-flowing—both top to bottom and bottom to top.

In a company I once ran, we had to write off $250 thousand in accounts receivable because the finance department notified the customer of pending legal action before informing the operations department. Had the operations department known before the customer was notified, we could have prevented the customer from reclaiming his assets until he paid the outstanding balance.

As a leader, you must create an environment that encourages full disclosure of information without fear of retribution, as well as healthy and vigorous debate that doesn't get so overly critical that creative ideas are squelched. How do you create this type of healthy, free-flowing environment for communication? It's not as hard as you might think.

Discuss the Most Important Things Most Often

Everyone needs to know the company's most critical objectives—from top leadership down to the line worker. Everyone should be able to articulate what business you're in, the top objectives for the current year, and their personal alignment with those objectives. To lead everyone to this point of understanding, stay on message. Talk often about the things that matter the most. This is an extremely effective way to gain alignment.

Open the Door

The old "open door" policy goes a long way toward helping leaders and workers clarify information so that people can do their jobs and meet their objectives. There's no quicker way to lose touch with an organization than to close your door to write memos and send e-mail. Get out and talk to people, and stop sending e-mail to people who sit right next door. Trust is built one-on-one, eye-to-eye, not in electronic relationships. Sometimes we solve problems faster face-to-face when we don't have to deal with repetitive memos and e-mail.

Another reason to keep your door open is that employees are forever misinterpreting the subtlest actions that managers would never dream they even notice. When you close your door, here's what they're whispering: "I wonder what's going on in there? Is he getting canned today? Is she getting a raise instead of me? What are they hiding from us?"

Employees come up with the strangest stories about what's going on behind closed doors. It's all fear of the unknown, so don't shut the door for arbitrary reasons, and if you do, be aware of how it might be interpreted. Full visibility and full disclosure, to a point, are good rules to follow. The obvious exception is when you are discussing confidential information, including performance reviews.

When people drop in, be prepared to handle the interruption skillfully. Get to the point quickly by asking what's needed. If it's simple, provide the information and end the conversation. If it's more complicated, ask the person to schedule a time to discuss the issue, since you are currently involved in another important matter and can't give the issue your full attention. The key is to handle the matter quickly and get back on task. If not, your day will be consumed with interruptions and you'll get little else done.

One last point: when people skip over their manager to meet with you, let them tell you what's on their mind. Once you understand the issue, ask if they have already spoken to their manager before coming to see you. If not, ask why. If they have, ask why they need your involvement. Not only might you be able to solve the issue, but you will also gain some insightful information about your culture and potential areas for improvement. Handled right, these can be useful growing experiences. Handled poorly, employees will no longer seek you out for fear of reprisal.

Be Free with Your Own Ideas

One way to encourage an open, communicative environment is to be free with your ideas. The more information you disclose, the more information people are willing to give to you. It's a leader's role to begin the process. A good way to do this is to speak often in front of employees and field questions. When answering questions, give enough information to ensure understanding. Ask people what they think about certain ideas. Get them involved and feeling like an insider.

Think Before You Speak

Though you do want to be open, remember, as a leader, everything you say and do is under constant evaluation. Employees are following your lead, so you have to be certain and thoughtful of what you say. Whether you like it or not, your words will translate into action.

Employees want to please leadership, so an idea or a thought that you offer will be taken as a request. After you've left the room, resources will be marshaled to make that thought or idea reality. So think things through before you say them. If you're just throwing out an idea to brainstorm, say that in advance—and again before you leave the room.

Unfortunately, in some venues, you can't just speak extemporaneously because of either the audience makeup or the need to precisely communicate a specific point. In these situations it's important to prepare your thoughts in advance, and always take time to put things into perspective so people better understand the topic in the right context. This minimizes miscommunication and reduces false starts. At the same time, don't belabor issues. You have to find the right balance.

Body Language Speaks Volumes

Nonverbal cues are very powerful. Your body language and demeanor will strongly influence how people interpret your words. Sometimes what you don't say has more influence than what you do say. The unfortunate thing about this less obvious way of communicating is that you often don't know that people are making these judgments in a microsecond. Regardless of your words, people will interpret your actions. If you're not alert, you may not know this until the wrong results show up! Some of the classics include appearing ready to respond before hearing out the other person, lack of eye contact, keeping your arms folded, and shrugging your shoulders.

Be Hard On Performance and Easy On People

Another way to promote free-flowing ideas is to monitor the type of criticism you hear in meetings. It's fine to be hard on performance—you should be, when numbers, quotas, commitments, and objectives are at risk or go unmet. But you don't want to be hard on people. Watch your language. Don't make it personal. Instead, focus on the business problem. Also, be careful not to shoot the messenger. This will help people feel as free to talk about where they are failing as where they are succeeding. When there is a need to deal with a performance problem, do it privately. If you don't, your people will clam up.

Practice Conversation for Action

There are two types of conversations in business: information sharing and what I call "conversation for action." The first is a great way to stay connected, spawn creativity, or debate. The second focuses on producing results. It's request driven and specifically involves asking someone to deliver something by a certain time. It's detailed down to the deadline: I need X by Y. And in some situations, there is no room for negotiation.

Conversely, you should be listening for answers that are commitment based—either "I can do that" or "I can't." If the answer is "I can't," then an effective leader will focus on the roadblocks by asking the person what he or she needs to meet the request. An answer of "I can't" or "I'll try" without specific reasons is unacceptable.

You must be direct. There's no room for vagueness in a business geared for action. Often leaders hem and haw because they fear directness will be interpreted as either uncaring or intimidating, when neither has to be the case. To the contrary, directness often makes people feel more comfortable because they know exactly what's expected of them. Direct requests help people perform and prioritize. It's also important to provide ample opportunity for questions to ensure complete understanding.

Ask for Verification and Feedback

For your most critical requests, make certain that your communications are direct and clear. Then ask the person or group you're addressing to repeat the request and instructions. This might sound obvious, but it's one of the best ways to avoid being misunderstood. If they can accurately feed your message back to you, you've done your job well. There are plenty of challenges in business. Don't create additional ones by leaving important items to chance.

Another technique for getting more informal feedback is to allot time at the end of meetings for general discussion. People like to have a few minutes just to talk about the issues that were reviewed. This is an effective way to gain collaboration and alignment, as well as to clarify the "how" part of getting things done. Since the right people are already together, it's easier to solve issues and get commitments then instead of having to coordinate schedules later.

You also might want to ask people what they think about an idea—both the good and bad. Generally speaking, people enjoy providing input. Asking for feedback, either directly or through general discussion, is an excellent way to minimize surprises and avoid problems. When problems arise, it's important that they surface early and people are made aware of them so corrective action can be taken and negative outcomes are minimized.

Trash the Hidden Agenda

The more direct and unambiguous you are, the more people will know what you expect of them and the greater the chance for achieving your objectives. Success is not measured at the end of the year by determining who has decoded your secret desires and somehow solved your riddles. Success is based on your ability to tell people clearly what you want up front, so that everyone can win.

Employees' fears escalate when they don't believe "what you see is what you get." If they think there is an ulterior motive or hidden agenda, everyone will fail. So it's important that you communicate thoroughly enough that people feel you are giving them all the information you have. After all, they are the ones who have to execute on your direction.

The same holds true when you are asked questions. Make your answers as direct and specific as possible. People are uncomfortable with vague responses. If you are not at liberty to answer, tell the person you can't and don't make up excuses. If you have a hidden agenda, it's a little like sending someone off with half a map and hoping they find the destination.

I remind clients that getting their employees on board at the beginning through effective communication saves time spent having to round them up later. It's also important to connect results with previous communications to show how they are directly linked. This is a great credibility builder. People remember what you say, and they are searching for continuity. Make certain you provide it.

Be a Teacher

A powerful aspect of effective communications is teaching. Yes, leaders must also teach. Your organization needs to grow and learn. So when making requests, take extra time to explain why.

This seemingly simple extra step yields two important benefits. First, it puts the request in a larger context, which increases the probability of it being done right the first time. Second, it teaches the organization how you think, which strengthens alignment and shortens the decision-making process.

We've all worked on teams where we didn't have to say much and everyone just "got it." These are high-performance teams where each team member fully understands how other team members think. This type of understanding doesn't come on day one. It's built over time through logic and lots of explaining why certain requests are being made. This phenomenon explains why leaders entering a company from the outside often bring team members with them. They need this high level of understanding to perform effectively. They need to be able to exchange information at an almost telepathic rate.

This is a very high level of executing for results through excellent communications, and it's extremely difficult to achieve. However, those teams fortunate enough to perform at that level are able to dramatically increase the amount of time they can devote to planning, strategizing, and moving the company ahead.

Ask Why, Why, and Why Again

When serious problems arise, another effective communications tool is to ask why three times. You do this to quickly find the root cause of the problem and avoid wasting resources that address only the symptoms. Once you begin communicating this way, real problems—and solutions—will surface quickly. Employees will quickly understand that they will have to answer why something has happened three levels deep into the problem.

For example, they will know that you will ask why the primary objective was not met. Once you have the answer, ask why a second time to ascertain why that happened. Finally, when you have the second answer, ask why one last time. You will only have to do this questioning a few times before everyone begins dealing with the real issues. Employees will anticipate your levels of questions and craft concise explanations of how objectives were not met and, more importantly, what to do to get back on track. But if some people can't answer why, ask them to find out and to follow up with you. This is no place for guessing.

Take Talk for a Walk

There's no better way to stay in touch with your organization than to take frequent walks around the company and listen, ask questions, and observe. This is not management by wandering around, but purposeful visits to ensure that all employees understand how they contribute to achieving the company's top objectives. If you don't schedule time to do this, you won't do it, and avoiding this responsibility can lead to big problems. The objective is to look for and ensure alignment between the company's stated objectives and what people are actually doing. To accomplish this, you need to ask only two questions: What are you doing today to help the company achieve its objectives? What one thing could we do to make your job easier?

By asking these questions, at a minimum you will learn whether there is a communication breakdown between leadership and the people doing the work. It's all about alignment. People should only be working on the most important company objectives. They should know what they are working on, how they're going to achieve results, and how to tell you what they need to make their jobs easier. Sounds like common sense. But it's not common practice.

Take this purposeful walk at least a couple of times a week. Don't plan where you're going ahead of time, just block out the time and do it. Don't announce your plans in advance. Show up in places you haven't been. Go to the loading dock. Go to the customer service desk, accounts payable, or the manufacturing floor. It only takes twenty or thirty minutes to find a few people you haven't talked to in a while and ask them those two questions.

When a company's top leaders start doing this, the management team down the line will typically start modeling the behavior. This heightened level of interaction will give you an instant status report on the state of communications in your company. You will be amazed at what you learn.

While working for a Fortune 500 company, a senior executive asked my advice on what he could do differently to improve his effectiveness. After thinking for a moment, I said, "One morning, while you're in the elevator on the way up to your office on the eleventh floor, close your eyes and randomly hit the button for another floor. When the door opens, get out and meet some of your people, because they don't know who you are." It was a risky but honest statement, and more executives need to hear the same message.

He thanked me for the suggestion and tacitly agreed. Unfortunately, agreeing and doing are two completely different things. I offered this particular action because he was making ill-informed decisions without involving the right people. My hope was that he would consider including other people in the decision-making process. Ultimately he stuck with the status quo, continued to make poor decisions, and was eventually demoted. Thankfully, in this case, the president had the courage to take action instead of leaving this individual in place or shuffling him to a lateral position.

When conversation happens between an executive and a line worker, it generates profound, far-reaching effects. It's motivational for everyone in the company to believe that they can talk directly to a company executive who cares about making their job easier. It makes everyone believe that what they're doing is important. It is!

Taking your talk for a walk also allows you to identify areas for improvement. Eventually you will see the same people surfing the

Internet or taking breaks instead of working. Don't avoid these people. Instead, tell them you realize you've not effectively communicated what's important in this business and how they contribute. Let them know that they're part of the company for a reason, you're counting on them, and you can't allow them to waste their time. Take responsibility and ask them why they are not engaged in productive work. Maybe they don't have enough to do. If that's the case, then involve their manager and solve the problem.

There are only a few reasons that people are unproductive. They either don't know what's expected of them, they need training, they're in the wrong job, or they need to go. Be careful not to confuse efficiency with unproductivity. Some people get things done so well they have time available to handle more. Whatever the reason, it's management's responsibility to address the situation immediately.

Every minute of unproductive time ravages profitability. Be certain to inform middle management of your findings and ask that they address problems systematically. If you don't see signs of improvement during future walkabouts, it's time to look deeper into the ranks of middle management.

Talk to People You Don't Have to Talk To

Another way to talk to people you don't normally have contact with is to host skip-level meetings with people who don't directly report to you. If you are an owner or senior leader, meet with middle management and frontline workers. These can be casual meetings over lunch, with you in your best listening mode, or you can ask to attend a meeting impromptu. When you do this, I strongly suggest just being an observer.

Remember your purpose: You're verifying alignment and finding out what stands in the way of the organization achieving its top objectives. You're not there to take control or to get people to like you. Instead, you're assessing the culture to determine what changes are required. You are part of the mechanism that ensures top objectives flow throughout the company. This technique will give you tremendous insight into how you can fine-tune every part of your company.

Realize that this behavior will intimidate middle management. Their irrational fear is that people below them will say things to senior management that will jeopardize middle managers. The common fear is that someone will make them look either ignorant or wrong, or possibly deliver bad news that they want to contain up the ladder.

Typically middle managers work hard to spin bad news in a way that makes them more comfortable, when in fact unfiltered information is the most useful. When you see this happening, get to the root cause, and find a solution fast. This type of behavior can quickly cause complete communication chaos. Remember, your job isn't to solve all the challenges yourself; it's to identify where improvements are required and to hold management accountable for making them. If your middle-management team is afraid of your holding skip-level meetings, find out why. It's your responsibility to drive fear out of the organization.

Don't Fear Bad News

Ineffective leaders often get stuck in the habit of only delivering good news. Don't be afraid of bad news—it's a business reality and an essential component of clear and effective communications. When you talk about things that go wrong, it makes you even more credible when you share the good news. This often comes up when it's time to review financial performance or deal with difficult customer situations. Remember that every employee wants to know how healthy the organization is, and it's your role to communicate that in a way that is understandable, digestible, and forthright.

If your bad news is likely to be on the ten o'clock news, it's even more important for you to be the one to tell employees first. Sometimes this is impossible, either because the information is privileged or legally can't be shared in advance of public disclosure. If this happens, hold a general conference with your employees as soon as possible, even if that means a conference call at midnight. Clear the air and answer questions. People can handle bad news if you tell them about it early. Explain why the situation occurred, what's being done, how it impacts them, and how they can help.

Talk About Compensation Is Not Taboo

Another subject that often gets swept under the rug is compensation. If you don't communicate about your compensation structure and benefits, employees will create their own reality, and, generally, it will not be as positive as the truth. So if you want employees to support your objectives, they must not be the last to know what's going on with raises, bonuses, or benefits. Look for general forums where you can communicate major changes so that everyone hears the same news at the same time. In large companies, closed-circuit television and Web casts can be a solution. In smaller companies, hold a meeting in the break room. Figure out a way to involve employees working off-hour shifts and in satellite offices, various regions, and different time zones.

This doesn't mean you have to address individual pay or specific increases, but you can let people know that the benefits plan is fully funded, that the employee benefit contribution will increase, or that the company is doing well enough to participate in bonus plans or profit sharing this year. Let everyone know that compensation is linked to performance, both the company's performance and individual performance. Then reward each employee based on whether they meet their own objectives. Compensate people who contribute the most the best. It's that simple. And you can make that known across the company without talking specifics.

Pay Special Attention to Middle Management

The biggest potential for a communication breakdown is generally in middle management. The senior people, particularly individual owners, have the clearest vision of what they want to accomplish, and they want everyone to embrace their vision. When there are only a few levels, it's relatively easy to accomplish. As the number of levels and employees grows, communication becomes more difficult.

Pay special attention to middle managers when you walk around the company. Observe how members of management work among themselves. In meetings, are managers openly offering their help to one another? Are they openly sharing ideas and resources? Or do they spend more of their time defending their shortcomings or tooting their own horns? In their conversations, do they talk about the company's success or their own? Are they also out interacting with their employees, asking questions, and checking for alignment?

If you don't witness free-flowing information and sharing of resources, then middle management is probably building walls to prevent effective communication from trickling down. When this happens, take action. You can't afford a breakdown in this critical area.

Listen to the Little Guy

A big part of being a great communicator is being an excellent listener. When ideas or criticism come from a lower level, listen even harder. Workers on the front lines often know more about what's going on in a company than anyone else. Be careful to listen to a whole idea or rationale before you shut someone down and start giving your own version of what's going on. Be careful not to criticize too soon, or you'll quickly be labeled as a leader who only wants to hear good news or is a know-it-all. Soon, yes-men will surround you, and there goes truth.

Listen for Victim Mentality

As a leader, you must be attuned to communication that promotes a victim mentality. If you're hearing excuses, you've got victims. Here are some common victim excuses: "I couldn't get it done because the other department didn't . . ." "It's not my responsibility." "I'm not paid enough to be proactive." "I don't have enough resources." "We've tried that before and it didn't work."

The best way to break out of this negative cycle is to ask why three times. If this doesn't work and the conversation wanders into excuses, get back on course with one question: What do you need to accomplish your objective? Stay focused there, and employees will have no room for excuses.

Listen for Those Who Love the Sound of Their Own Voice

We've all been a part of organizations where there are people who need to comment on every item, even when it's not in their arena. These are the people who love the sound of their own voice. Be sure to minimize this type of conversation. Otherwise team members who should be talking will often get distracted and lose interest. When one individual stalls conversation, bring it back to the center by letting everyone know that the conversation needs to focus on what must happen to accomplish objectives. If the same people continue to distract the conversation, call them on it.

ACTIONS TO TAKE NOW

To help improve your communication abilities, please list your responses to the following:

1. What are the three most important ways you can help improve communication in your organization?
2. How do you know important information reaches everyone in the organization in a timely and accurate manner? If you're not certain, distribute a short survey to find out.
3. Do employees at different levels think they can communicate directly with you about anything they think is important? If not, what can you do about it?
4. How often do you travel around your organization and speak with people you either don't know or don't usually see?
5. Do employees consider you a straight shooter, or do they think you have hidden agendas? If the latter, how can you change this perception?

Now that you better understand how communication functions as the critical path to executing for results, it's time to focus more closely on what you should be communicating. Tracking and measuring are integral parts of progress. In the next chapter, you'll learn more about establishing ongoing evaluation and measurement in order to maintain and increase your gains.

TEN

Measure What Matters Most

Complacency is your worst enemy.

After you capitalize on The Five Attributes of Highly Profitable Companies and your company is operating at a high level of efficiency and effectiveness, it's time to push harder. Complacency is the worst enemy of profitability because as soon as you think you've found the keys to the kingdom, someone changes the locks. You can never put too much distance between yourself and your competitors.

The world around you constantly changes. To survive and prosper, prepare your company to morph. The people around you, the processes you've created—even your top objectives—have to be resilient enough to adapt at a moment's notice. Your operating plans must have variables ready to set in motion when you detect the need to shift gears.

So how do you know when it's time to alter your action plan? You monitor key progress metrics, watch your competitors, listen to employees, ask clients questions, challenge the status quo, and remain open to new ideas. The best way to prepare for change is to equip your business with an early-warning system that signals when it's time to take corrective action. The earlier you can identify a problem, the better prepared you are to deal with it or avoid it and maintain profitability.

Your early-warning system constantly keeps your business in check. It doesn't have to be complicated or rigged with bells and whistles. Instead, key metrics tell you if your company is on plan.

The key metrics will tell you instantly how well you're executing against plan. You can't wait forty-five or sixty days after month's end for numbers. That's too late to correct your course. Think of your early-warning system as a thermostat, always taking in information, comparing it to the goal, and making real-time adjustments to achieve the desired result. The more timely and accurate the information, the easier it is to adjust and act. We all know it's a lot harder, and sometimes impossible, to catch up than it is to make minor adjustments along the way.

Follow a few basic principles when creating your key metrics. First, fewer are better. Each leader should track only the significant few metrics that pertain directly to the organization's top objectives. Second, the key metrics must be easy to understand and interpret. You should be able to read them at a glance. Put them in graph form, and color-code them so that trends and deviations pop off the page. That way you'll know immediately the precise action to take if something shows up red or yellow or green. When the color changes, replace debate with action.

Following is a guide for creating an early-warning system for your company or organization through a number of key metrics that will gauge your performance according to The Five Attributes of Highly Profitable Companies. To obtain a copy of the early-warning tool I use in my workshops, please go to www.bobprosen.com/earlywarningtool.

Superior Leadership

Having a vision and making the strategic decisions required to achieve it are the key components of superior leadership. But to take the risks required to be a superior leader, you must have accurate information, a culture based on ownership and accountability, and an understanding that people are your most important asset. The following key metrics and guiding principles will help you achieve the attributes of a superior leader and keep your business on track.

1. **Make Sure You Have the Right People in the Right Positions** On a regular basis, mentally run through your direct reports and evaluate whether or not their best assets are being properly used in their current positions. Use the following checklist:

    - Are results on plan?
    - Do you have to follow up to ensure that things get done?
    - Are commitments made and met?
    - Can you trust each team member with sensitive information?
    - Does each person know more about their area of expertise than you do?
    - Do people actively request help and proactively offer solutions to solve problems?
    - Are you provided real-time information and performance metrics?

2. **Develop a Succession Plan** You must have a succession plan so you can quickly replace your most important people. Keep it updated, because change is inevitable and often unpredictable.

Know how you will operate in the interim between the time someone leaves and the time they are replaced. Have your key people provide a concise plan that outlines how the organization will operate effectively in the event they depart or are gone for an extended period of time. Review these plans and know which members of the management team you will temporarily depend on to share responsibilities.

3. **Make Results Visible** Post results throughout departments, in break rooms, the cafeteria, and on the company intranet. Establish a visible measurement system to facilitate a self-correcting process. Each business unit or functional area should have its top objectives and current performance posted and updated for all to see. This makes it simple for managers to discuss with employees how their specific actions contribute to the achievement of their unit's top objectives.

4. **Eliminate Ineffective Meetings** Some meetings are essential. Others are a huge waste of time. To ensure you don't have too many of the latter, require all meetings to have agendas with a clear purpose and agreed-upon, documented action items—not minutes. People will applaud when you make this mandatory. They would much rather do something valuable with their time than sit in a meeting where nothing is being accomplished. The payoff is real, so shift gears now. I strongly encourage leaders to randomly pop into meetings strictly as an observer to make certain change is underway. Occasionally ask to see agendas and the action item log.

5. **Implement Conversation for Action** To know that team members are holding each other accountable, listen. Are team members regularly asking one another for commitments? Are they talking about what actions will be taken to achieve results?

6. **Effectively Utilize Rewards and Recognition** Ensure that rewards are disproportionate and highly visible. Those who achieve

the most get rewarded the most—and everyone should know that. It's just that simple. Have managers show you their people's performance and compensation compared to their objectives. Ensure that people at the bottom are either improving their performance or being moved out. No one with poor performance gets to remain on the bottom for more than a year without action being taken. And that includes your managers.

7. **Review Your People Report** Track vital human capital results on a monthly and year-to-date basis. The report should include the following:

   - Total head count compared to budget. Include part-time and contract employees.
   - Number of new hires by functional area. Include the hiring department, source, title, compensation, and the reason they joined the company.
   - Number of people who left the company. Include the reasons why each person left and whom they worked for. This information has to be obtained from a third party, such as human resources. If you're losing the wrong people, find the root cause and eliminate it.

8. **Make Time to Plan** This one is easy to assess. How much time each month do you spend planning compared to doing and reacting? Set a goal and hold yourself accountable. If you're falling short, look to your other metrics for answers. A shortfall could mean one or all of the following:

   - You don't have the right people in the right positions.
   - Your organization's objectives and responsibilities are not clear.
   - You are not delegating effectively.
   - You are not focused on your company's significant few top objectives.

9. **Hold Frequent Communication Forums** Talk to everyone it affects when you have news to share, and schedule time to walk around your company to ensure alignment and root out process issues.

Sales Effectiveness

Meeting the top line by generating revenue is my definition of sales effectiveness. It's the fuel that helps you accelerate around obstacles and gets you across the finish line. The following key metrics and guiding principles will keep your sales organization on track. All metrics should be tracked and reported monthly and for the year to date. Depending on your business, your company might require more frequent reporting.

1. **Revenue** The following are the most important booked revenue metrics to track:
    - Total booked or actual revenue compared to plan, by line of business, geography, product, and service
    - Total gross margin and contribution margin compared to plan by line of business, geography, product, and service
    - Average selling price compared to plan, by product and service
    - Average billing rate per hour compared to plan
    - Product and service revenue compared to quota, by salesperson
    - Product and service revenue by channel compared to plan
    - Product and service revenue generated by other internal departments compared to plan. Sources include inside sales, customer service, project management, and operations
    - Total discounts and credits by salesperson, product, and service

- Average sales cycle by product and service
- Change in revenue split between existing customers and new customers

2. **Volume** Track units sold to ensure that the correct product mix and associated margins are being achieved. These are the most important metrics to track:

    - Total unit sales by product line compared to plan
    - Total hours billed by line of business and by project compared to plan
    - Total units and hours sold by salesperson compared to plan
    - Total units and hours sold by channel compared to plan
    - Total units and hours sold by other internal organizations

3. **Customer Churn** Keep track of the number of customers gained and lost. This information provides tremendous insight into your company and deserves the attention of all senior management. Measure the following:

    - Customers gained, by source
    - Customers lost, by reason
    - Average length of customer relationship
    - Change in average annual sales volume, by customer

4. **Revenue Forecast and Sales Pipeline Management** Regularly check the accuracy of your pipeline forecast by comparing what was projected to close against what actually closed during the month. You want these numbers to be relatively close to one another. If they aren't, take action to determine the root cause and fix the problem. An effective sales process has defined steps or gates that have to be completed before closing probabilities can be accurately assigned. The key is to have this process in place and hold sales management accountable for using it.

Be careful not to confuse revenue sold with revenue recognized. If you forecast closing a multiperiod deal next month that has either milestone payments or a monthly recurring component, you might not be able to recognize all the revenue at the time the deal closes. Don't allow revenue definitions and recognition rules to impact your forecast accuracy. Do the following instead:

- Compare revenue recognized to revenue forecasted by product and service, and by salesperson.
- Account for how the company recognizes revenue in the forecast.

5. **Long-term Contracts** Track the average length of new contracts and structure your compensation plan to encourage sale of long-term contracts as long as required margins are maintained. Long-term contracts improve forecast accuracy and reduce the cost of sales while increasing the quality of your revenue stream.

6. **Sales Productivity** These are the most important numbers to track by salesperson:

   - Number of meetings with decision makers
   - Number of proposals presented
   - Number of deals closed
   - Year-to-date revenue and margin compared to plan
   - Number of wins, by reason
   - Number of losses, by reason

Operational Excellence

To remain competitive and flexible, you must know the cost of doing business. This is where margins are maintained and efficiency is gained. Many companies pay too little attention to this important area of business and unknowingly allow profits to erode. Use the following key metrics to control costs and bolster profits.

1. **Cost Management** All expenses should be compared to plan and any deviations analyzed. Underspending in a certain area can be just as critical as overspending. For example, underspending in essential education or research and development can have a far-reaching impact. When revenue is under plan, you would expect costs to follow suit. In this scenario, it's important that costs are sufficiently under plan in relation to revenue, and therefore, they also require review.

2. **Head Count** Because people are typically a company's biggest expense, have a complete understanding of all the people components. Don't allow yourself to overinvest in this category. It's very difficult to get back on plan, and in many cases, layoffs will be inevitable if the top line underperforms for any length of time. These are the key people metrics:

   - Total head count by department, including part-time and contract employees compared to plan
   - Total head count by level and by department compared to plan
   - Fully loaded cost of people compared to plan
   - Overtime cost by department compared to plan
   - Average revenue per employee
   - Average margin per employee

3. **Lost Profit** Track the number of hours given away to customers. You need to know why every potentially billable service is given away. You can't repeatedly give value away and make your required margins unless you incrementally charge for it or include these costs in your price. Once you start giving services away, it's difficult to charge for them. Here are some of the hours that are often given away:

- Maintenance above the contracted amount
- Product or upgrade support
- Problem resolution, especially for issues unrelated to your product or service
- Project scope creep

4. **Productivity** These are perhaps the most difficult metrics to quantify and track. Operating budgets assume certain efficiencies and productivity gains. Therefore, those same units of work must be measured in order to compare results to plan. Understanding productivity by department and function enables you to confidently adjust your workforce according to changes in revenue. One of the most important tools for accomplishing this is an effective time or labor-reporting process. Labor reporting, coupled with units of work, provides the information you need to manage and improve productivity. These numbers are critical when you're deciding what to automate, how growth will impact business, or when to stop functions that add no value.

5. **Inefficiency** Companies throw millions of dollars of profit away every day because they don't have defined processes in place to eliminate unnecessary costs and increase profitability. To eliminate these costs, begin by capturing the volume and cost by category. Then list the categories from most costly to least costly and from highest volume to lowest volume. Next, select the largest cost and highest-volume categories, apply RCA and ICA, and watch your profitability increase. Here are a few categories to consider:

   - Service calls
   - Customer complaints
   - Spoilage and waste
   - Warranty claims

- Returns
- Missed due dates
- Service interruptions
- Overtime

Once you decide on the categories to measure, graph the volume and cost associated with each category over several weeks or months. You'll suddenly see the ones costing the company the most. Use RCA and ICA on the top offenders to eliminate the root causes, and then move down the list.

6. **Project Management** Another area to watch closely is your company's ability to effectively manage projects. The two most important project metrics are *completed on time* and *within budget*. One of the best ways to track these is to compare percentage of work complete to plan and percentage of budget spent to plan on a monthly basis. This enables you to quickly determine all projects that are behind schedule or over budget. In either case, action is required.

Financial Management

Your finance team should provide you with the information you need to make timely and well-informed decisions. Use the following metrics to minimize surprises and stay ahead of your competition.

1. **One Page** Have your finance team give you one-page, color-coded monthly financial reports that clearly show all budget deviations, who owns them, and what's being done to remain on plan. With these reports, you can review the health of your company in minutes instead of spending hours wading through numbers and reports. When data is turned into information, you have more time for planning and decision making.

2. **Cash Flow** Every month, or if necessary, every week, or even daily, review cash flow to see how much cash came in, where it was spent, and exactly what was retained.

3. **Profit by Product or Service** This should be in graph form so it's easy to compare actual profit to plan, spot deviations, and track trends. Companies often complain about the lack of systems to compute product profitability. My answer is to hold finance accountable for providing this information.

4. **Accounts Receivable** Don't allow your company to become a bank for your customers. Aggressively manage collections. This is a black-and-white rule. Sympathy should not affect receivables in any way. On the front end, finance, in conjunction with sales, is responsible for credit screening to ensure that customers are able to pay their bills. Track receivables in the traditional categories: 0–30 days, 31–60 days, 61–90 days, and 90+ days.

   The key is to capture the reasons why every account moves from 89 days to 90 days outstanding. Determine the top reasons, and use RCA and ICA to eliminate the root cause. Watch your receivables go down. Enforce all contracts with provisions for charging interest and late-payment penalties.

5. **Billing Accuracy** Too often, companies don't consider the impact their billing system has on their customers. They don't think of billing as a meaningful way to communicate with their customers when, in fact, it is. Track the number of bills in dispute and short pays and the number of refunds being made. Then make sure your finance team can show you how they are using RCA and ICA to eliminate these problems.

6. **Project Audits** You must know whether or not each project yielded the expected financial results. Compare actual results to what was promised. If the results committed to were not achieved, find out what went wrong and adjust the approval

and monitoring process. Remember, don't approve project investments unless you can track performance.

At one company I joined, we didn't have a standard project-approval process. As a result, projects were undertaken without fully understanding the cost and profitability. Most projects involved software development, which is notorious for coming in late and over budget. To solve this problem, we developed a standardized "deal sheet" that had to be completed and approved by the appropriate organizations, including finance, in advance of contract approval. This allowed the company to objectively evaluate projects to determine if they made operational and financial sense or if any terms had to be changed prior to approval. In addition, this change allowed us to conduct accurate post-project audits to ensure the approved ROI was actually achieved.

7. **Financial Forecasts** Hold your financial team accountable for projections. Were they accurate? If not, why not? Your finance team should provide a monthly business report that shows performance against the most important financial objectives, as well as recommended changes to remain on or get back on plan. Business leaders can decide if they want to follow those recommendations or not. It's up to finance to outline problem areas and suggest specific action. Finance, in conjunction with business leaders, should also provide a three-month rolling financial forecast to keep the senior management and external constituencies informed.

8. **Real-time Information** Finance must provide accurate, real-time information. Notice I did not say real-time data. It's unacceptable to present financial information one or two months after month's end. Finance is also the keeper of all results information, including asset utilization, inventory turns, raw material costs, accounts payable, financial ratios, and head count. Finance is also responsible for deviation analysis. The finance

team should explain why the company is ahead of or behind plan. To accomplish this, they have to constantly test budget assumptions against reality. That's the way to determine whether they remain valid or require revision.

9. **Early-Warning System** Develop an early-warning system to help minimize risk and financial surprises. To get a copy of an early warning tool, visit www.bobprosen.com/earlywarningtool. You know the things that impacted your business over the past few years, whether positively or negatively. Track them going forward so that you might be able to avoid problems and capitalize on changing conditions. You might also want to track the factors that had the largest impact on your clients' buying habits.

   - Market growth
   - Your company's growth
   - Number of new and exiting competitors
   - Number of customers gained and lost
   - Number of customers filing for bankruptcy
   - New product introductions

10. **Planning Process** Finance should administer the entire planning and review process. Expect this team to keep you on course by publishing a planning schedule with milestone reviews at monthly, quarterly, and year-end points. Think of your finance team as the master of ceremonies, making sure people come to the table with the information required to develop and review their operating plans.

11. **External Reporting and Filing Dates** Finance is responsible for staying current on all regulations, such as generally accepted accounting principles and Financial Accounting Standards Board regulations, and other industry-specific requirements, as well as meeting all required public filings and due dates.

Customer Loyalty

Having reliable products and services and creating trust by meeting commitments and practicing proactive communication are instrumental in achieving customer loyalty. Almost half of your competitors don't even measure customer satisfaction, let alone customer loyalty. Here are the important metrics.

1. **Customer Surveys** Implement a measurement process via mail, e-mail, in person, or over the phone. It's important to conduct these surveys using a third party or someone inside the company who doesn't have day-to-day contact with your customers. To get a free survey template that includes the two most important questions for determining how loyal your customers are, go to www.bobprosen.com/loyaltysurvey.

   Here are a few of the areas to evaluate:

   - Effectiveness of your sales team
   - Effectiveness of your support staff
   - Quality of your products and services
   - Value of your products and services
   - Ability to meet commitments
   - Level of responsiveness

   For your largest and most important customers, I strongly suggest engaging a professional firm to conduct in-depth telephone or in-person interviews. Retaining your top customers is critical. You can't afford to wonder if they're loyal.

2. **Track Results and Take Action** Use the same survey questions each time to develop reliable trends. Graph trends and compare to plan. Isolate the biggest problem areas and take action to minimize them. Your goal is to increase loyalty over time. Take the results seriously and don't rationalize. Hold your team accountable for improvements.

3. **Referenceable Customers** The goal is to have 100 percent referenceable customers. If you shoot for anything less, your results will be lower. Meet quarterly to review all clients who are not referenceable and identify the reasons why. Isolate the top reasons and take action to improve the results.

4. **Contract Renewals** Develop a monthly report showing contracts that are up for renewal at least six months in advance. Track renewal results monthly and identify those at risk. Assign ownership to any contracts at risk and hold people accountable for the renewals.

5. **Churn** Know how many customers enter and leave your company each month and why. This is an area where you might need to dig deep for the truth. I suggest a report showing the source of each new customer and the reasons why any customer leaves. Make certain you are satisfied with the results. If not, assign accountability and eliminate the root causes. The goal is to retain 100 percent of your profitable customers, capitalize on new customer sources, and bolster internal processes to halt undesired attrition.

6. **Refund and Credit Report** Have a monthly report showing the amount of refunds and credits your company issued, by reason. Determine the root causes and eliminate them.

7. **Top Account Status** Each month, hold a short meeting to review the status of your most important customers. The objective is to minimize surprises and retain your top customers. I suggest using a green, yellow, and red color-coded report to highlight status for the most important areas, which include the following:

   - Billing accuracy
   - Volume of trouble reports
   - Competitive threats

- Outstanding proposal status
- Changes in key decision makers
- Need for executive involvement
- Topics of concern

8. **Problem Resolution** Track customer-impacting problems by category. Your goal is to eliminate repeat problems and solve problems quickly on the first call. This information is easy to obtain and should be viewed in chart format so that you can see improvements over time. Have leaders monitor customer service calls and report their findings.

9. **Proactive Communications** Your company should have a defined process in place to proactively contact your clients at a moment's notice. This is important for two reasons. First, you want to be able to minimize surprises by informing clients of upcoming events and providing them with advance notice of issues or changes before they impact their business. Second, proactive communication enables you to stay top-of-mind with your customers and lets them know what you're doing for them behind the scenes. This is an effective way to build value and differentiate yourself from your competition. Accomplishing this requires the following:

    - Up-to-date and accurate customer contact information
    - Procedures for providing information using e-mail, direct mail, phone calls, or Web portals
    - A process to approve critical messages before sending
    - A process for contacting dissatisfied customers
    - Approved standardized reports that inform customers of additional behind-the-scenes work your company performs on their behalf

With your measurements and early-warning system in place, you should have all the information you need to make informed business decisions. Remember that metrics and measurements are just tools. Think of all of this information as if it were pieces of a puzzle. You still have to put the puzzle together. It doesn't replace judgment and wisdom, decision making, or results. When your early-warning system alerts you to problems, address them immediately. Never just monitor a problem to see if it's going to get better. The majority of the time, it will only get worse.

The most effective way to use this information to improve performance and consistently achieve your objectives is to implement a formal operations review process. When I was leading organizations, I always required monthly operations review meetings to ensure the organization consistently achieved its objectives. The purpose of the meeting was to review top objectives and metrics so that resources could be allocated wherever improvements were needed.

The secret to those meetings was to focus exclusively on deviations to plan. All business unit leaders followed the same format, using charts and graphs to show results against plan for each objective. Following each chart was a concise set of bullet points that clearly stated how positive deviations would be maintained along with actions already underway or soon to be taken that would improve results enough to achieve plan. This was not a problem-solving meeting. It was, however, the place to ask for assistance or to accept offers for assistance. If you follow this format, not only will results improve, but you will also reduce the time you spend reviewing results.

This is the exact process I followed at the Internet hosting company I led to yield a 28 percent reduction in operating expense, 100 percent improvement in customer satisfaction, and 36 percent earnings improvement while maintaining the top line through the largest market decline in history.

I used the process again at Sabre to improve profit 51 percent, close more than $100 million in new sales, and exceed our profit plan by 38 percent. We also used it to meet our accounts receivable target and achieve the company's highest billing and utilization rates. Today I show clients how to apply these tools and tactics to boost their bottom line and achieve results that count.

ACTIONS TO TAKE NOW

Take a few moments to turn inward so that you can address the following:

1. Are you a good listener? Do you learn about or sense problems the first time you encounter them, or must they be brought to your attention several times before you acknowledge them and act?
2. Do you have a few, vital metrics identified, and are results available to you when needed? If not, what steps will you take to accomplish this?
3. Do you have an effective early-warning system to minimize financial surprises? How will you create one or improve the one in use?
4. List the top three areas of inefficiency in your organization and what you will do to improve them.
5. List three ways that you can improve your ability to help employees execute for results.
6. Do you do a good job of holding people accountable so that they get agreed-upon results? How can you improve in this area?
7. Who are your top people, and what are you doing to retain them and increase their loyalty?

Even the most successful companies can be dethroned. If you're on top, you can bet your competition is working to beat you. This brings us to our final lesson: how to maintain the gain and stay in the winner's circle by truly sustaining high-performance profitability.

ELEVEN

Maintain the Gain

Remain on course.

Whether you're already in the winner's circle, on your way to profitability, or still struggling along the way, this chapter unites everything we've covered into a powerful model for sustaining and accelerating high-performance results and profitability.

At one time or another every company gets off track. When this happens to successful companies, however, they recognize the problems and get back on track quickly. There are a number of common reasons a company is pulled away from its mission:

- The company grew too fast and couldn't keep up with all the change.
- With success, leaders became removed from daily operations without ensuring adequate talent and controls were in place.

- Key leaders have changed without sufficient bench strength behind them.
- The company has gone through a major change, such as a merger, acquisition, or a significant reduction in force.
- People are in the wrong positions. Either they don't have the right qualifications, or they've been given something to do that they aren't capable of doing.
- Priorities have changed without the appropriate review and approval process.
- The organization is confused because there is a lack of clear understanding of what needs to be accomplished.
- The leadership team has not anticipated risks or identified obstacles to overcome, so they're stuck.
- Managers aren't asking one another for help and, instead, are thrashing around getting little done.
- The culture is suffering from victim mentality. People are blaming the system, the process, their colleagues, and anyone and anything instead of taking ownership of the problem.
- Ownership has not been clearly assigned, and action items start falling through the cracks because what one person took as a commitment, others didn't.
- The organization has grown sloppy during times of plenty.
- The penalty for missed commitments has waned.

So, if you've strayed off course, how do you get back on track and into the winner's circle?

The single most important thing a leader can do to institutionalize success is to reestablish the organization's top priorities, put the right people in the right jobs, with clear objectives and measurements to track performance.

Assign ownership to people who know the business even better than you do, and require them to focus on the significant few objectives. Too often, companies lose focus because they take on too many responsibilities and spread themselves too thin.

Be clear about what you're asking people to do so that you eliminate false starts. People want to accomplish tasks, so you have to give them the right direction. Give them objectives derived from deep thinking, not a half-baked idea. When you communicate clearly, make requests of people, and get commitments, you will make progress. It's as simple as telling people what you want, as well as why and when you want it.

You must also have a measurement system in place to track progress on all of your top objectives. These measurements act as an early-warning system that brings leadership together to reprioritize and take corrective action when the landscape changes.

Finally, you must discover the root cause of every problem so that you don't waste valuable resources fighting the same problems time and time again. This inefficiency generates unnecessary costs and prevents companies from focusing on what's most important to move them forward and accelerate profitability.

Now let's break this line of thinking down according to The Five Attributes of Highly Profitable Companies.

Superior Leadership

A superior leader must avoid a number of pitfalls to institutionalize the success of a company. Ask yourself the following questions to ensure that your leadership skills are up to the task and tuned for continuous high-performance profitability.

1. **Does the Company Have the Right Top Objectives, Supported by the Entire Senior Management Team?** Start here before looking any deeper. If there is any uncertainty in this area, everything else is at risk.
2. **Are You Keeping People Focused on Achieving the Company's Top Objectives?** Don't be surprised if you're met with blank

stares when you walk around your company asking people what they're working on to achieve their organization's top objectives. It's actually quite common for people not to know either the company's most important objectives or how what they're doing fits into those objectives—or both. Determine how far the communication breakdown reaches by asking people if they're aware of new products, the company's earnings, recent customer wins, or key leadership changes. Ask people who the company's most important customers are.

When you detect a problem, fix it. Find where communication broke down and ensure that those responsible know what to do better in the future. Work more closely with your management team so that they know how to consistently communicate objectives. Ask the manager responsible for the team experiencing communication problems to develop a one-page action plan explaining how they're going to fix the communication gaps. Then hold them accountable. People need to know you're serious about this.

Visibly post the company's most important objectives so that everyone knows them and is reminded of them every day. Scrutinize middle management, which is the primary communication body in any company. Make sure your middle managers meet regularly with both senior managers and with their own teams to discuss progress against their objectives. To monitor communications, attend skip-level meetings with employees who are not your direct reports.

3. **Are You Managing People Too Closely?** We all know how uncomfortable and frustrating it is to be managed too closely. So when you're in a leadership position, check your style. If you're too involved, back off, and learn to delegate. Let people do their jobs. After all, if you have hired smart, your people know what to do to succeed. However when the organization is far off course, it's time to roll up your sleeves and get as involved as

necessary until you're confident the situation has been corrected. After you've stepped away, apply this test: Are people performing according to your expectations?

If not, address the problem. You have to be fair and equitable to the whole staff, and it's neither fair nor equitable for good people to be burdened with the incompetent. When you need to make a personnel change, do it. Cut the dead wood. Don't rationalize, procrastinate, and end up doing nothing.

4. **Are You Helping People Prioritize Actions in Alignment with the Company's Most Important Objectives?** Everyone wants to do it all, but in reality, you can't. So when you find that your team leaders are failing to meet objectives, help them determine where they are spending their time. If too much time is focused on items other than the company's most important objectives, help them triage the list and give them permission to stop doing a number of tasks. This is easily accomplished by having each person track their time for three days. Have them group like items and review the results with you. You'll quickly see where adjustments need to be made.

5. **Are You Helping Managers to Be Effective in Their Meetings?** Pop into meetings and listen. Are people solving problems and talking about things they need to do to move the company forward, or are they focused on complaints, excuses, and extraneous issues? If the latter is true, explain to your managers how to effectively conduct meetings focused on achieving the company's top objectives and hold them accountable for immediate improvement.

6. **Are You Watching for Team Members Who Are Focused Internally, Not Externally?** Be keenly aware of negative politics between peer groups. It will show up in e-mails, in meetings, in the hallways, and in break rooms. When you hear team members talking about "what's best for me" instead of what's best

for the company, nip it in the bud. Address it directly by telling the person to immediately discontinue this type of political behavior and to stay focused on what's required for the company to achieve its most important objectives.

Go a step further and require team members to ask for and offer help instead of criticism. Let everyone know his or her behavior needs to be focused on the success of the team, not the success of the individual. That being said, you still need to recognize individual performance and success in context with how it supports the company's goals. Celebrate and reward top producers for their above-and-beyond efforts and achievements.

7. **Are You Asking People What They Need to Be Successful?** This should be a regular question in your day-to-day conversations with employees. When you ask someone to do something and give them a deadline, you also should ask them if they have everything they need to make that deadline. If not, deal with it immediately. When people fail to meet objectives or deadlines, ask what specific actions you can take to achieve the objective. What's required from others?

   Typically, you'll get realistic answers to these questions and learn a lot about your company while teaching people how to remove roadblocks on their own.

8. **Are You Watching for Busywork?** Pay special attention to staff and other corporate functions, such as accounting, human resources, and information systems. Are they engaging in nonessential work and generating unnecessary reports instead of actions that support the company's top objectives?

   If so, how do you root out busywork and put it permanently to rest? Ask your P&L and business-unit leaders to annually evaluate the effectiveness of the support they receive from each central staff or headquarters department. Ask them to list what they want the staff or department to continue doing, stop doing, and start doing. Then take action and hold the leaders accountable.

9. **Have You Run Out of Time to Plan?** Are you always running to keep up? Are you missing commitments because you're in too many meetings? Are you predominantly reactive instead of proactive? Do you regularly take vacation or are you carrying it over year after year? Does everyone seem to come to you for answers? Then chances are the devil is in the details. It's time to release some of those details.

   The higher up you are in a company, the fewer decisions you need to make. If you're at the top of the corporate ladder, you should only be making the decisions that have the biggest impact on the business. If you're involved in small decisions, you're not working on the right things. Here's how you fix it:

   1. **Determine your top priorities.** There should only be three or four. Write them down and keep them on your desk so you won't get distracted.

   2. **Delegate, delegate, and then delegate some more.** Remember, delegation is not the same as abdication. You don't just turn your back. Stay involved at appropriate points until your goals are realized. Obviously, if you have hired smart and surrounded yourself with pros, delegating effectively is pretty easy.

   3. **Perform a three-day time study.** Write down where you're spending your time for three days and, at the end of those three days, assess yourself:

      - Are you spending time on too many things that aren't priorities?
      - What types of activities are taking more time than they should?
      - Where are you gravitating in the business?
      - Is that the best place for you to be spending your time?
      - What issues are coming to you that shouldn't?

Be brutally honest with yourself and make whatever adjustments are required. Be certain to communicate those changes to your team, or they won't understand why you're doing things differently.

After you reprioritize, block out time on your schedule for planning and for thinking about the Big Picture and the Next Big Thing as they relate to your business. If you don't schedule it, you won't do it.

Sales Effectiveness

To supercharge your sales effectiveness, there are a number of pitfalls to avoid and systems to have in place.

1. **Don't Tolerate Hockey-Stick Forecasts Where Revenue Is Projected to Substantially Increase Toward the End of the Year.** You can't allow your organization to end up way off plan at the end of the year. Don't let your sales team continue to forecast success further and further into the future with the hope of taking up all of the slack by year's end. It rarely happens.

2. **Require Weekly Results Reviews.** Work from a concise agenda that moves quickly through comparisons of actual results to plan. Don't accept excuses. If it's in the forecast, it must be delivered. This will teach people to accurately assign probabilities throughout the selling process. The same holds true for revenue left off the forecast. Don't allow sandbagging. All revenue opportunities must be included on the forecast.

3. **Don't Underestimate the Value of Marketing.** Even though many businesses have a great idea or product, if they don't have an effective value proposition and tools in place to communicate that value proposition to the correct target market, they won't end up in the winner's circle. The key is to hold marketing responsible for delivering quantifiable results.

4. **Scrutinize Your Sales Team and Weed Out the People Who Don't Sell.** This sounds obvious, but you'd be surprised how many companies suffer because they allow people who just can't sell to remain in sales. In addition to quota attainment, one of the best ways to figure out who should stay and who should go is to travel with some or all of your salespeople and watch them in action.

5. **Don't Let Your Sales Team Tell You Week after Week That They Can't Make Their Numbers Because of Poor Customer Service, Product Quality, Slow Delivery, or Any Other Excuse.** Listen to them and quickly address problem areas, but don't allow excuses to stand as roadblocks. Commit the organization to removing legitimate roadblocks so all that remains is the salesperson's ability to sell.

6. **If Your Sales Team Consistently Comes Up Short of Quota, Take a Hard Look at Your Product or Service.** Is it up to date? Is it inferior to others on the market? Involve your marketing team to help sales understand the competition and the marketplace. Equip your salespeople with the best tools, training, and support so that they can effectively differentiate and sell your product or service. Require your sales manager to develop a concise action plan to meet quota, and hold her or him accountable. Ultimately, it's up to the sales manager to deliver results.

7. **Don't Allow Your Salespeople to Live Off Annuities.** Their job is to constantly create new customers.

8. **Let Your Salespeople Sell.** Don't burden them with many internal nonselling responsibilities, or they'll leave or spend time on non-revenue-producing activities.

9. **Require All Wins and Losses to Be Shared Across the Entire Sales Team.** Doing this enables the transfer of knowledge,

development of best practices, success replication, and the incorporation of lessons learned.

Operational Excellence

Watch for these basic trouble signs when you're working to achieve and sustain operational excellence:

- Hazy understanding of your cost structure, including what drives expense in the business and who the owners are for each cost component on the P&L
- No effective RCA/ICA process in place
- No plan for automation to increase productivity and reduce costs by eliminating human error
- Expenses and overhead that are out of control
- Budget owners who can't factually explain deviation from plan and who don't proactively take action to realize the plan

What are the solutions for these operational trouble points that will help you accelerate profitability to new levels?

Scrutinize Every Dollar Spent

First and foremost, hold finance accountable for providing information to show how all business costs are allocated, including direct costs and variable costs by product, by line of business, even by customer and location, if appropriate. The formulas used to create these models need to be understood by all so that, when these costs hit the P&L, you don't spend time arguing about the numbers.

A full understanding of your cost structure also requires knowledge of how costs vary relative to changes in revenue. Costs in various areas of your business may or may not grow in proportion to revenue, so you have to look for economies of scale along the way. Talk to cost-center owners. Determine how much work can be absorbed without increasing the cost structure, and start from there to increase efficiency. Before increasing personnel, for instance, ask cost-center owners to automate certain functions and to stop doing less important work. If you're not comfortable with the answers you're getting, consider implementing a time-reporting system to determine where people are spending their efforts.

During budget reviews, scrutinize all costs. Any requests for increases should go through a strict justification process to demonstrate how the cost increase will directly benefit the top or bottom line, improve customer service, or increase your competitive advantage. If they can't be justified, don't approve them.

Listen and Learn from Every Complaint

Take an RCA approach to every customer complaint or service problem. When you eliminate the root cause, you also eliminate costs associated with these problems, and profitability goes up.

Study Your Competition

Especially when pricing becomes an issue, it's imperative to understand your competition. You either have to be a lower-cost producer or provide significant differentiation so that your customer is willing to pay a premium for your product or service.

Ultimately, though, the biggest winner is the company with the lowest cost structure. If your cost structure is higher than your competitors', devote resources to figuring out why. You want to obtain all of the competitive information you can in every legal way possible. After all, the company with the most intelligence and the ability to translate and execute on that intelligence will win more business and enjoy higher profits. There's a reason they call it competition!

To gather competitive intelligence, leaders will want to assume some of the following actions themselves and delegate some to others in the company, including managers and people in sales, marketing, and customer service:

- Ask questions of your customers to see if they will give you information about your competitors' products, services, pricing, and support. Depending on your relationships, many times they'll accommodate your request. The more dissatisfied a customer is with your competitor, the more willing they'll be to share this information with you.
- Attend your competitors' seminars, product announcements, or programs. If they screen you out at the door, so be it. A lot of times they won't, and you'll be getting great information.
- Become a competitor's customer in a limited way to test products, services, and pricing firsthand.
- Call and ask questions of their sales and technical staffs. Technical people in particular love to talk about their company's products and services.
- Read about them. Find every piece of public information that's written in newspapers, magazines, on the Internet, and on their Web sites.
- Hire some of their best people, particularly those without a noncompete or where the noncompete has expired to ensure that the employee is not bound by certain restrictions to the other organization. But be careful. You want to avoid lawsuits and keep your competitors from raiding your team in retribution.
- Visit their booths at trade shows and collect as much information as possible.
- Talk to your competitors' customers' procurement staff, and ask what they like best and least about their current products and services.

- Your competitors' suppliers may also be a good source of information.
- The flip side of this, of course, is that your competition may be doing all of this to you. Educate your people about how to screen out competitors' attempts and keep proprietary information confidential.

Financial Management

The trouble spots to watch for in terms of financial management include the following:

- Inaccurate forecasts
- Data without recommendations on how to improve
- Surprises and no early-warning system in place
- Too many unforeseen prior-period accounting adjustments
- Lack of leadership in the planning and financial review process
- Determining if projects yielded committed returns
- Getting the month's results forty-five or sixty days after month's end. Being relentless in this area will pay off!
- Expenses incurred without the proper signatures or approvals
- Customer credit problems caused by inconsistent or ineffective credit screening
- Too many unforeseen external audit findings
- Weak control systems
- Too many late or revised public filings

Communicate Accountability

To keep your financial management team focused on accelerating profitability, make certain the team understands its critical role. If they're falling short, then chances are you've not communicated well. Your finance team must do all of the following:

- Lead the planning and review process, including establishing and publishing a schedule for the development of operating plans and budgets, as well as weekly or monthly progress reviews.
- Follow up consistently to ensure that periodic financial reviews occur as scheduled.
- Recommend ways to get back on track to each line organization that is off plan.
- Implement effective financial controls.
- Establish and be the keeper of an early-warning system.
- Work with internal organizations to define and redefine reports so they are in a format that's useful.
- Increase accountability and reduce debate by listing the data source, time period, and creator on each report.
- Label each report—a simple up or down arrow will do—that immediately identifies whether the news inside is good or bad.
- Eliminate all unnecessary reports by asking recipients how each report helps them achieve the company's most important objectives.

To establish an effective early-warning system, your finance team has to look back before looking ahead. By reviewing the last one or two years or a time when results were exceptionally good or bad, you can arrive upon key performance indicators. The goal is to identify specific changes that occurred in your business environment that directly correlate to past results. Once these indicators are identified, finance can use them to develop an early-warning system that helps avoid problems and exploits opportunities. This is a great way to learn from the past and improve future performance. Some of the indicators you should be reviewing include the following: What was happening to your cash flow? What was happening to your margins? Had any new competitors entered the marketplace? Had any competitors left? Were clients paying on time or late? What was happening with pricing? What was going on with inventory levels? Were there key personnel changes or excessive turnover?

The Role of Effective Audit Processes

Effective audit processes help identify actions required for improving results. For instance, finance should develop investment criteria so that every P&L owner has a standard template to follow when presenting projects for approval. Each project or investment should include specific standards for success and a way to measure it—whether by increases in customer satisfaction, sales volume, production capacity, automation, or quality improvement. Using this technique will eliminate debate about whether or not the project was successful.

Upon completion, every major project should go through the audit process so you can evaluate if desired results were achieved. Depending on the outcome, your finance team can refine the approval process to screen out losers and boost winners.

I also like the idea of posting the results of a company's top projects on a chart that includes a timeline and major milestones so that everyone in the company can see how the projects are performing on delivery and cost.

The audit process also helps you identify the people who've achieved top results for the company. That way you can properly reward and recognize them. Then you can look to these people to lead the next project, knowing you can rely on them to achieve its goals.

A Final Word on Processes

Every company is built on processes—people following certain procedures to get results. Finance should identify the key metrics required to measure process performance. Make certain manufacturing, customer service, product development, sales, billing, and other important processes have key metrics assigned to them. Be certain to involve process owners in determining the correct measurement to use in making sure the metric is logical, useful, and accurate. Remember, don't get caught up in process paralysis. Metrics are only enablers, a means to an end. The goal is to consistently achieve results that count.

Customer Loyalty

The trouble spots that help you identify problems with customer loyalty are obvious: Your customers are upset. They don't know what's going on. They're surprised by your actions. They're complaining that commitments aren't being met. As a result, you're losing customers, they're buying less, and you're not getting enough testimonials and quality referrals to gain new ones.

The Most Common Customer Complaints

Other than complaints about the product not working as promised or not being delivered on time, the largest number of customer complaints center around poor communication. The best way to remedy this situation is for customer service and sales to closely track complaints from all sources. If you lose a customer, perform an exit interview to find out why. If you lose a sale, require your sales team to find out why. Don't settle for opinions and vagaries. Know the facts.

Then communicate the valuable information that comes out of these negative situations to improve your business. Make certain the same problems don't recur.

There are many ways to communicate with your customers. Advise them of new products and services, when you win an industry award, or have a great quarter or year. Announce it—in the media, with a postcard, an e-mail, a phone call. No matter how you do it, let your existing customers be the first to know your good news. Don't be random about it. You need to have a plan in place to keep customers in the loop.

Whenever you're dealing with a dissatisfied customer, the best way to get things back on track is to make and meet commitments while overcommunicating relevant information. Keep your customers well advised until they ask you to do otherwise. That's your sign that you've succeeded.

When problems are severe, don't be afraid to bring in senior management. Your customer will feel especially important if you temporarily transition their account to a senior person until it's back on track.

Depending on the severity of the situation, be prepared to document a "get well" plan. Then provide the customer with a status report to help remove any ambiguity. There are lots of gray areas in business, so make as many of them as possible black-and-white. Use status-report meetings to secure customer sign-off on deliverables along the way. Using this method, you won't get to the end of the project and find out they're not satisfied.

On large, complex projects, develop a statement of work that includes clearly defined and mutually agreed-upon criteria for success. That way both parties know when to declare a project a success.

Act on Survey Results

Make certain you continue measuring customer loyalty. More importantly, do you know if your company is taking appropriate actions to improve results? Do the metrics bear this out?

Test your customer touch points by being a customer. Buy your own product. Call your help desk. Call customer service, complain, and see what happens.

Institutionalizing Success: A Final Word or Two

Finally, to help your company achieve extraordinary bottom-line results, you must establish, nurture, and protect the following essential components:

- Have a clear and concise value proposition based on consumer demand.
- Have clearly defined objectives.
- Hire people with a relentless, unyielding commitment to achieve, and reward them well.
- Build a culture based on accountability and focused on execution.
- Have accurate and timely metrics to evaluate performance.
- Encourage a free flow of uninhibited information.
- Remain flexible and adapt readily to change.
- Reward results, not activity.

Remember the greatest payoff of sustaining and accelerating high-performance results and profitability is that it provides your company with choices unavailable to the competitors you've left behind. With high-performance profitability, you will have the option to innovate. Best of all, high-performance profitability will bring you the satisfaction and pride that come from creating value and seeing your company and the people in it succeed.

ACTIONS TO TAKE NOW

To keep yourself and your company on top, here are some actions to take now:

1. List five ways that you can improve your leadership abilities.
2. What actions could you take to make your sales team more effective?
3. What actions are necessary to improve the operational excellence of your company?
4. What actions are necessary to improve the financial management of your company?
5. What needs to be done to encourage customers to become even more loyal to your organization?

By following the proven techniques that I've presented throughout this book, I know that leaders of business and not-for-profit organizations can do well as they also do good.

EPILOGUE

Beyond Profitability: Doing Good and Doing Well

Do you believe that you and your company can do good and do well at the same time? I do. I have written this book to give you the strategies and techniques to use daily to accomplish your goals profitably and ethically.

After reading this book, I hope you will share my belief that a highly profitable company can be both competitive and successful while maintaining its integrity. The old adage is true: You can do good and do well. With the attributes I've outlined, you don't have to cheat to become highly profitable. There's no need to color your reporting or "cook the books" to achieve great success.

Whether you are the leader of a Fortune 1000 company, the owner of a privately held business, the leader of a not-for-profit organization, or a manager or supervisor within a department, successful leaders share a set of common goals. We want to be part of a successful organization that consistently achieves its objectives. We want to make our work easier and more fulfilling.

We want all of our employees working collaboratively to achieve the organization's objectives, have fun, react less, and be proud members of an enterprise that is respected and admired.

We all want to be part of a company where employees look forward to coming to work and being part of a bigger mission. We want to create an environment where everyone's ideas and talents are sought after and respected, where trust is high and politics are kept to a minimum.

Unfortunately, some business leaders look for the quickest road to success, regardless of the consequences. The business pages of newspapers and magazines are filled with news about seemingly successful companies and CEOs who basked in the glory of the cover stories and feature articles, only to come crashing back to earth as their dishonest, corrupt, and greedy business practices came to light.

Companies can be ethical, fair, and socially responsible while competing fiercely to win in the marketplace. You can do good and do well—these traits are not mutually exclusive. Companies such as Edward Jones, The Container Store, Adobe, TDIndustries, JM Smucker, Chick-fil-A, and Southwest Airlines are just a few examples of corporate success achieved by doing both good and well. There are also many small and midsize companies and organizations, including Rasa Floors (owned by my good friend Michael Rasa), Junior Achievement, The Boy Scouts of America, and many others that have achieved exemplary status.

Private companies, public companies, and not-for-profit organizations share some common goals, including the drive to constantly meet their objectives, provide increasing value to their customers, hire and retain top talent, and succeed. They also have some very different ones. Why? Because they have different constituencies. Public companies have a financial responsibility to their shareholders to produce quarterly earnings that are in line with expectations. When earnings are not achieved, often shareholders are hurt the most. As a result, some companies focus excessively on earnings instead of improving their operations, making higher quality products, or investing in their people.

There also is a distinct difference between leaders of public companies and the company itself. Although many leaders own stock, they don't "own" the company. They are caretakers. It's easy to distance themselves from decisions because they and the company are not one and the same. This also holds true for many not-for-profit organizations. When times get tough, their leaders can leave, often with attractive severance packages and "golden parachutes." Worse yet, it's not uncommon for poorly performing leaders to remain in their positions too long instead of being "managed out" of the organization.

On the other hand, privately held companies, or more specifically the owners or founders of these companies, can't separate themselves from their enterprise. Whatever happens to their company directly impacts them. If the company does poorly, they do poorly. They take downsizing, pay cuts, and benefit reductions personally and with great angst. They can't leave when the going gets rough.

Although the level of personal commitment and the "why" might vary, all organizations are driven to win and achieve their goals. This book cuts across industries and categories to deliver proven answers and solutions that enable any organization to more easily and consistently achieve its most important goals.

Have you ever tried implementing something you thought was simple, and it ended up being a lot harder than you thought? Just think how hard it is to implement something that's complex. Sometimes it's impossible. I believe successful organizations understand the beauty of simplicity, so this is one of the themes I stress in this book. That is why I have outlined not only what to do,

> Organizations have the tendency to make things too difficult. There is a belief that for something to be good, it has to be sophisticated, elaborate, and complex.

but more importantly, how to do it, with exact guidelines and recommendations you can use immediately, without interpretation, to get real results that count.

Some of what you have read may be common sense. The real question is, how much of it is common practice throughout your organization, and how do you know?

Your company has been created for one purpose: to achieve a mission. To do this requires consistent delivery of results against goals. Results are best achieved when organizations have strong leaders who know how to balance vision and results, create an accountability-based culture, hire the right people, communicate effectively, realize that people are the most important asset, tie recognition and rewards to results, operate with integrity, and have the courage to lead.

To achieve success requires great leadership, vision, and the ability to execute, along with several other critical factors, including the following:

- **Market position:** being in the right market segments with a strong competitive advantage
- **Innovation:** being able to bring innovation to market faster than the competition
- **Balance:** being able to balance long-term and short-term priorities to remain profitable

These critical factors require constant attention from top management. When success in all these areas is achieved, you have the formula and ingredients for greatness.

Profitability in and of itself is not the ultimate objective. It's only the enabler. The real goal is to have choices.

Profitability enables organizations to have the freedom of choice. Organizations that operate with integrity and consistently achieve their financial and operating objectives are respected and admired. Their performance allows them to take better care of employees, customers, and shareholders.

Their reputation allows them to attract top leadership, employees, and board talent. They are also able to give back to society to help make the world a better place.

Years ago, while I was attending graduate school at Georgia State University, one of my professors told the class something that I have never forgotten. He said there are two great things that can happen to you in life. The first is to find what it is you really love to do. The second is to have the courage to go and do it.

Therefore, if I boil everything down to one nugget, it is this: Choose to do something in life that is more than just a job, that is something you love, that has meaning. I hope you are fortunate enough to do what you love, because it makes doing good and doing well that much easier.

This book is about doing. It shows you how to work smarter, not harder. Doing it right is a fulfilling, empowering, rewarding, and deeply gratifying experience. I believe we can all be members of this elite club. I am honored to share this information with you and expect that it allows you to achieve results that count.

If this book spoke to you, let me hear from you. Please share your challenges, triumphs, and inspirations by e-mailing them to me at results@bobprosen.com. I promise—I will read it! Until we meet again, remember this: you and your organization have the ability to achieve greatness.

Never give up!

APPENDIX

Keep Up the Momentum

- Free leadership effectiveness assessment online
- Custom training programs
- Expert business advice series
- Self-development materials
- Additional tools, references and *RESULTS* e-newsletter

The Next Step

In *Kiss Theory Good Bye*, you have the playbook to consistently achieve your objectives and out-execute the competition. The next step is to put these tools and tactics to use and take a closer look at your own capabilities within each of the five attributes. The following few pages will show you how to get started and where to get help.

I recommend that you begin by visiting www.bobprosen.com to participate in the free Leadership Effectiveness self-assessment, receive your profile, and instantly compare your organization's leadership effectiveness to other organizations across multiple industries. You can access the leadership self-assessment at www.bobprosen.com/leadershipeffectiveness. This self-assessment is designed specifically for leaders with direct reports. It involves answering a few simple questions and can be completed in less than ten minutes. When you've completed the confidential assessment, you'll have a clear understanding of how to begin your journey toward superior leadership.

Once you have an idea of what you need to work on, I suggest you develop a simple action plan. You may want to focus initially on the list of Actions to Take Now at the end of each chapter of *Kiss Theory Good Bye*. I can also personally help you jump-start your company or organization through high-value training programs and keynote speeches that give you the information you need to consistently achieve extraordinary operating and financial results.

Custom Training Programs

The Prosen Center for Business Advancement designs a custom program exclusively for your organization, and delivers it on-site or at a location of your choice in a time frame that fits your schedule and budget. The Prosen Center will teach you and your management team more strategies, tools, tactics, and secrets to help you execute and achieve results with certainty. These highly customized, company-specific programs are designed to identify and remove the roadblocks that inhibit your organization from realizing its critical objectives and true potential. Programs open with a private pre-event session with the top leaders to learn the current state of the business. Key leaders are interviewed to identify challenges,

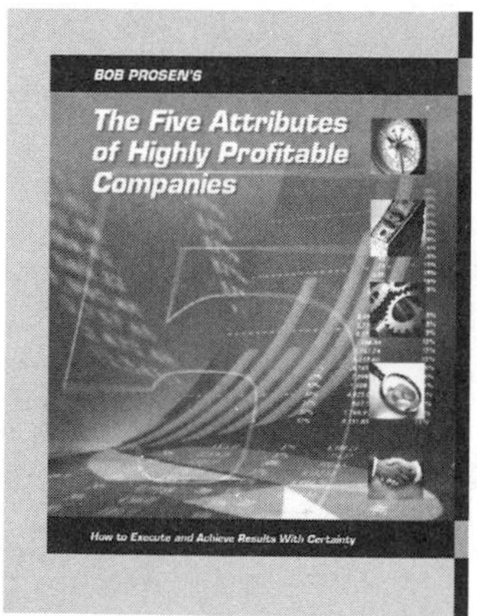

and a customized program based on some or all of the five attributes is developed. Within ninety days after the custom program, a follow-up session is held with the leadership team to review what was learned, how the team has acted on its advanced knowledge, what results have been achieved, and the measure of the team's buy-in and commitment to sustaining results.

The program delivers powerful tools and answers at high speed, with an economy of words and an abundance of examples that clearly guide you to personal achievement. And to underscore this one-of-a-kind learning experience, you'll receive a proprietary executive workbook that contains the exact tools used by the world's most successful companies to execute and achieve unprecedented operational and financial results. This valuable resource will help you execute better for years to come.

On completion of the program, you will have clear, piercing insight into how your organization can dramatically improve operating and financial results and deliver exceptional satisfaction to employees, customers, and share owners. You and your organization, whether it is large or midsize, will benefit from this highly interactive delivery of high-performance strategies, tactics, and tools never before revealed outside the corporate war room.

You'll learn how to

- Execute and consistently achieve your operating and financial plan
- React less and have more time to plan
- Increase accountability so you get the results you need
- Attract and retain top talent
- Eliminate rework and increase quality and profits
- Convert data into information to speed decision making
- Lock in customer loyalty
- Create an early-warning system that recognizes problems before they become severe
- Improve your productivity without increasing your effort

Who Should Participate? My program provides the greatest benefit to the following types of leaders:

- **An owner, president, CEO, and his or her senior leadership team** who wants to learn proven ways to execute, increase accountability, alignment, make your job easier, run your organization more smoothly, consistently meet objectives, and create more time to identify and act on what's really important.
- **Managers** who need to find better ways to achieve goals and increase accountability. You'll also learn how to align all of your employees so that they work efficiently on the right objectives, enabling you to have far fewer personnel situations to manage.
- **Board members** who need to expand their experiences. You'll learn proven techniques that can help the companies and not-for-profit organizations you advise better meet operating and financial goals.
- **High-potential leaders** who are ready to move up and who want the "playbook" for running a successful company without the waste of costly mistakes and learning from the "school of hard knocks."
- **Leaders under siege** who do not have time to waste and must act fast and effectively to achieve essential operating and financial results.
- **Leaders of a start-up or fast-growing company** who must move rapidly toward profitability while reducing risk and consistently achieving financial and operating objectives.

I know that your time is valuable and your need for results is paramount. That's why I've distilled twenty-five years of successful corporate leadership into a customized business-execution program that can change the course of your organization's future. This exclusive results-driven program delivers actions and answers that aren't available anywhere else. Prepare to engage in fresh, unfiltered discussions about what it takes to deliver extraordinary bottom-line results.

In addition, you will receive ongoing support with educational, teleconference, assessment, and newsletter information to help you consistently meet your business objectives.

What execution challenges are you facing within your organization? Now you can find the answers and secure the blueprint you need to help beat your competition and achieve exceptional bottom-line results. It's all part of this exclusive custom training program offered by The Prosen Center for Business Advancement.

If you're ready to improve accountability and results, schedule your leadership team today for this intensive, highly interactive learning experience that will return years of value to your bottom line. Call 972.899.2180 or visit us at www.bobprosen.com/workshop.

Welcome to the Expert Business Advice Series

As a business leader, you need immediate access to professional, reliable information and resources for many aspects of your business. You require dependable information that's easy to understand and instantly applicable to your issues.

Where do you go to get the answers you need on important operational, financial, legal, HR, contractual, technical, sales, intellectual property, business valuations, and other subjects? Until now there has been no comprehensive source that addresses the myriad issues facing today's business leaders.

That's why I have assembled leading industry experts to provide answers to your most important business challenges. This service provides you with specific how-to information you can use immediately and share with your organization.

The Expert Business Advice Series helps you conserve time and money so you can direct your efforts toward what's most important—thinking, planning, and leading your company forward. In today's fast-paced world, it's not only difficult to find qualified experts, it's also an expensive and frustrating experience.

Here is a sample of the topics available in the series, all produced by leading experts:

- **Wealth preservation:** How to structure and operate closely held companies to minimize transfer taxes, protect your family, and maximize wealth preservation.
- **Employment law:** Learn the latest inside tips from top labor experts that will save you time and money, and avoid lengthy legal hassles.
- **Intellectual property:** How to establish and protect copyrights, trademarks, patents, and licenses. When to use confidentiality and work-for-hire agreements.
- **Raising capital for start-up or emerging growth companies:** How to determine which type of capital is right for your business and how to locate and raise capital.
- **Wills, trusts, and probate:** How to structure your estate plan to protect your family and avoid costly probate disputes.
- **Secrets to hiring the right people:** The most important questions to ask before hiring someone, the best sources for obtaining top talent, and how to choose the right search firm and successfully negotiate terms.

The Expert Business Advice Audio Series is filled with critical information you won't find anywhere else. Best of all, you can create your own library and listen anywhere, while commuting, traveling, or even exercising! Become a subscriber today at www.bobprosen.com/expertadvice and start getting answers to your most pressing issues.

Superior Leadership: The Relentless Pursuit of Vision and Results

Superior leadership is the first of The Five Attributes of Highly Profitable Companies, and this CD is the perfect companion to what you've just learned. In this audio program, I coach you one-on-one about the most important aspects of leadership. You can check in anytime you want for a quick review, shot of willpower, or a fresh dose of inspiration. And you can listen anywhere, at any time, so you'll never forget your focus or lose momentum.

Whether you're a business owner, corporate leader, senior manager, supervisor, or someone in search of effective leadership training, my *Superior Leadership: The Relentless Pursuit of Vision and Results* provides the answers you need to achieve results that count. You'll learn the most important aspects of leadership as they apply to achieving extraordinary operating and financial results. You won't find any soft science or touchy-feely information. Instead, what you get is hard-hitting, straight-to-the-point information you can use to enhance performance in any type of leadership situation.

Here's some of what you'll learn:

- How to make your job easier and your organization run more smoothly
- How to hire and retain top talent
- How to react less and have more time to plan
- How to increase accountability and results
- How to align the entire organization in meeting your top objectives
- How to build loyalty and trust

Put these proven practices to work for you and watch the response you get from colleagues, superiors, and employees. Order the *Superior Leadership* CD today at www.bobprosen.com/superiorleadership.

How to Make Marketing Indispensable: An Inside Look at What Top CEOs Expect from Marketing

With years of experience, I know what business leaders want from marketing. This inside information will allow you and your marketing team to gain a seat at the planning table instead of being considered a discretionary expense.

Ever wonder why when budgets get tight, marketing programs and personnel get cut, whereas top salespeople always seem to keep their jobs? Why not marketing? Now you can discover the previously undisclosed rules of the game that will dramatically increase your value and importance.

Here's some of what you'll learn:

- How to become indispensable by linking your programs to the company's top goals
- The two most important alliances required to get your programs adopted
- What sales really wants from marketing
- How business leaders measure their marketing organization's effectiveness
- What CEOs expect from marketing

Whether you're leading a marketing organization, owner of an agency, a business executive in search of more effective marketing, a marketing student, or someone with the ambition to lead a marketing team, the *How to Make Marketing Indispensable* CD is for you. Order today at www.bobprosen.com/marketing.

Resources

You can further develop all of The Five Attributes of Highly Profitable Companies or just focus on one area with these tools and resources.

Superior Leadership

To enhance your leadership skills and learn how top-performing teams increase accountability and consistently deliver bottom-line results, go to www.bobprosen.com/superiorleadership

for information about my Superior Leadership CD, titled *The Relentless Pursuit of Vision and Results.*

For some of the most creative and effective ways to reward employees, refer to Bob Nelson's book *1001 Ways To Reward Employees.*

To participate in my free confidential online Leadership Effectiveness Self-assessment and instantly compare your organization's leadership effectiveness to other organizations across multiple industries go to: www.bobprosen.com/leadershipeffectiveness. This survey is designed specifically for leaders with direct reports.

Operational Excellence

To get a better understanding of the quality improvement tools used to reduce errors and rework, visit www.vanderbilt.edu/Engineering/CIS/Sloan/web/es130/quality/oldtool.htm.

Sales Effectiveness

Customer relationship management (CRM) applications are essential to manage relationships in an organized way. Review top solutions for small and midsize businesses at www.crm2day.com/news/crm/113673.php and www.2020software.com/default.asp.

One of the top CRM solutions for midsize businesses is SalesLogix, by Sage Software (http://saleslogix.com). It is designed specifically to help manage and forecast opportunities and retain and develop profitable, enterprise-wide relationships.

When it comes to contact management, task management, and forecasting solutions, three of the best sales force automation solutions are ACT by Sage software (www.act.com/), Salesnet (www.salesnet.com) and salesforce.com (www.salesforce.com).

To learn more about sales force automation solutions, compare quotes, and select your best option, visit www.buyerzone.com/marketing/sales_management/buyers_guide1.html?click=1.

Hoovers provides business information on twelve million public and private companies worldwide, including company profiles, financials, contact names, and competitors. To access information requires a membership subscription. Go to www.hoovers.com/free/.

Harris Information provides more than two million records for finding new customers and quality sales leads and includes business databases, business directories, and research reports. To access information requires a membership subscription. Go to www.harrisinfosource.com

Dun & Bradstreet provides information on ninety-two million businesses worldwide, of which 80 percent are U.S. businesses with ten or fewer employees. As a paid subscriber, you get access to company financial records, telephone numbers, executive names and positions, addresses, and credit-worthiness on both public and privately held companies. Go to www.dnb.com/US/index.asp.

Financial Management

For a list of some of the top business system software solutions for small, medium, and large companies, go to www.2020software.com/default.asp.

Microsoft Business Solutions also offers a suite of products designed specifically for small businesses which integrates with Microsoft Office. Go to www.microsoft.com/smallbusiness/products/mbs/sbm/detail.mspx.

Microsoft Business Scorecards Accelerator allows companies to simplify creation and management of Web-based, interactive scorecards to gain real-time insight into business trends, measure corporate performance, and enable faster, better decisions. It also supports custom-built scorecards and provides a means for consolidating analysis data from multiple sources. Go to www.microsoft.com/office/solutions/accelerators/scorecards/resources.mspx.

To get a free copy of my *Early-warning Business Tool*, designed to help organizations spot trends, learn from past performance, and more accurately predict future outcomes, go to www.bobprosen.com/earlywarningtool.

Customer Loyalty

For a comprehensive list of top customer and employee satisfaction survey software, go to http://directory.google.com/Top/Computers/Software/Marketing/Surveys/.

To get a free copy of the survey I use to evaluate customer loyalty, go to www.bobprosen.com/loyaltysurvey.

General

My *RESULTS* e-newsletter delivers proven business management advice along with answers and information you can use immediately to lead your organization to extraordinary operational and financial results. There is no "blue sky theory" in *RESULTS*. This bimonthly e-newsletter delivers tangible, valuable information to boost your organization's performance. To get your free subscription today, go to www.bobprosen.com/signup.

To get information on a wide variety of automated solutions applicable to multiple industries, with heavy emphasis in manufacturing, go to www.managingautomation.com/maonline/directory/Software.

Send an email to me at gift@bobprosen.com
and I will send you a valuable free gift.

How to Reach Us

The Prosen Center for Business Advancement
results@bobprosen.com
www.bobprosen.com
18352 Dallas Parkway, Suite 136427, Dallas, Texas 75287
Phone: (972) 899-2180 Fax: (972) 899-4813
www.kisstheorygoodbye.com

I look forward to hearing about your success and welcome your suggestions and questions. I promise if you send it we will read it!

INDEX

Words of Wisdom from *Kiss Theory Good Bye*

"Face reality; never rationalize.

Realize that at the beginning of the day, it's all about possibilities; at the end of the day, it's all about results.

Be hard on performance and easy on people.

Make commitments promises.

Be there on time and dressed to lead.

Think "responsible to you," not "responsible for you."

Know your unique selling proposition.

Ask why, why, and why again.

Solve root causes, not symptoms.

Don't major in minors.

Think "the significant few" versus "the important many."

Practice triage and stop doing less important work.

Reward results, not activities.

Get out of your office or get lost in your company.

Know when to shut up and close.

Replicate success.

Remove the obstacles and let your people perform.

Hire people who are smarter than you.

Think, "How do you know?"

Fire unprofitable customers.

Predict the future.

Get information, not data.

Get recommendations and answers, not excuses."

"Do not put a cap on sales compensation.

Encourage less talk and more action.

Send thank you notes.

Be a healthy skeptic.

Trust, but verify.

Delegate, don't abdicate.

Know that there's no such thing as too profitable.

Know that you can never have too much good information.

Trade farmers for hunters.

Ask, "How may I help you win?"

Upgrade from satisfied to loyal.

Sentence all of your profitable customers to "life."

Combine leading with managing.

Play as hard as you work.

Keep an extra pen handy for the next hundred bonus checks you'll sign.

Solve problems quickly.

Always do what's right for the company.

Hire smart or work hard. It's your choice.

Feel comfortable saying, "I'm taking two weeks vacation. You're in charge."

Know that anything is possible.

Do good, and you'll do well.

Never give up."